CORNELL STUDIES IN CIVIL LIBERTY

ROBERT E. CUSHMAN, *Advisory Editor*

Loyalty and Legislative Action

Loyalty and Legislative Action

A SURVEY OF ACTIVITY BY THE NEW YORK STATE LEGISLATURE

1919-1949

★

Lawrence H. Chamberlain

Dean of Columbia College

Cornell University Press

ITHACA, NEW YORK, 1951

Reprinted with the permission of Cornell University Press

JOHNSON REPRINT CORPORATION
111 Fifth Avenue, New York, N.Y. 10003

JOHNSON REPRINT COMPANY LTD.
Berkeley Square House, London, W. 1

Preface

THIS volume is one of a series made possible by a grant from the Rockefeller Foundation to Cornell University. For three years a group of scholars working individually under my direction have studied the impact upon our civil liberties of current governmental programs designed to ensure internal security and to expose and control disloyal or subversive conduct. The research has covered the work of federal and state "un-American activities" committees and the operation of federal and local loyalty and security programs. The first report, published in 1950, was *Security, Loyalty, and Science,* by Professor Walter Gellhorn of the Columbia University School of Law. This dealt with the problems of government-imposed secrecy in scientific investigation and the loyalty and security clearance procedures applicable to government scientists. Other volumes in the series include one on the House Committee on Un-American Activities, by Professor Robert K. Carr of Dartmouth College; one on the President's loyalty program and the summary dismissal statutes, by Miss Eleanor Bontecou, formerly an attorney in the Department of Justice; and a general survey of state programs for the control of subversive activities, by several scholars working under Professor Gellhorn's editorship. A final report will summarize the findings of the entire study.

In addition to these more general volumes the series includes studies of the control of subversive activities in three separate states. *The Tenney Committee,* by Edward L. Barrett, Jr., Professor of Law at Berkeley, tells the story of the famous California committee on un-American activities. *Un-American Activities in the State of Washington,* by Vern Countryman of the Yale Law Faculty, reviews the work of the Canwell committee in that state. The present volume by Lawrence H. Chamberlain, Dean of Columbia College, recounts and analyzes thirty years of legislative control of subversive activity in the state of New York.

Legislative committees set up to ferret out "un-American activities" have been bitterly attacked for ruthless invasion of civil liberties and warmly defended as patriotic and effective defenders of the public security. The purpose of Dean Chamberlain's study is to report accurately and objectively how the legislative committees set up to deal with subversive activities in New York have actually behaved, and what legislation has resulted from their work. Such honest reporting is vitally necessary if the thoughtful citizen is to appraise soundly the policies and procedures of such committees and form an intelligent opinion on how, if they are to be continued, their work may be improved.

The volumes in this series state the views, conclusions, and recommendations of the individual authors. There has, of course, been consultation and discussion among the group engaged in the entire study. Valuable aid and criticism has been received from a number of distinguished persons outside this group. Each volume, however, remains the work, and states the opinions, of the person who wrote it.

ROBERT E. CUSHMAN

Cornell University
Ithaca, New York

Contents

LOYALTY AND LEGISLATIVE ACTION

Introduction

IN *Free Speech in the United States,* Zechariah Chafee remarks that probing committees seem indigenous to New York. The first one, he points out, was created in 1780 to detect and defeat conspiracies of Loyalists. Professor Chafee was writing with special reference to the activities of the Lusk committee in 1919–1920. Since that time two additional New York legislative investigations of seditious or subversive activities have been added to the record.

Thus thirty years have produced three legislative investigations of "subversive" activities. All have devoted some attention to the schools, but only the last concentrated upon the schools. During the same period legislative concern over dangerous activity on the part of employees in governmental or educational institutions has found expression in other ways. The exclusion of the five Socialist members of the New York Assembly in 1919 followed closely on the heels of the Lusk investigation; and from the short-lived Lusk laws of 1921 to the Feinberg Law of 1949, a number of legislative proposals of one kind or another have been directed at the suppression or elimination of dangerous persons. Most of these proposed measures have been aimed at teachers or other educational employees. Many of the proposals have not been enacted but several have, the most important being the Ives Loyalty Oath

Law of 1934, the Devany Law of 1939, and the Feinberg Law of 1949.

No other state has shown so continuous a sense of insecurity. Why has New York been so obsessed with the specter of disloyalty? No wholly satisfactory answer has been discovered, but certain factors that may have something to do with it are suggested.

The New York Legislature is dominated by upstate influences. Most of the investigations have concentrated upon New York City. Rural suspicion of metropolitan conditions might therefore be a factor. Supporting this hypothesis are certain partisan factors. In general, Republicans have shown most enthusiasm for these investigations and have been most active in their prosecution. Both the Lusk and the Rapp-Coudert investigations were conducted by Republicans, and Republican support in the legislature was almost unanimous. Such opposition as existed or developed came from Democrats—usually New York City Democrats. Republican governors were, if not more enthusiastic than their Democratic counterparts, at least less disposed to oppose this type of activity. Both Governor Smith and Governor Lehman vetoed legislation aimed at "dangerous" teachers, whereas Governor Miller gave full support to the Lusk bills and Governor Dewey found no reason to veto the Feinberg Law.

The point of partisanship should not be pressed too far, however, because the loyalty issue has not been a party matter, and in actuality so much crossing of party lines has occurred that the question is badly confused. No one showed more antipathy to the action of the New York Assembly in 1919 than former Governor Charles E. Hughes, an eminent figure in the New York Republican Party. In fact, the New York City Bar Association, a group in which prominent Republicans exercised dominant influence, strongly condemned the Assembly for the way it handled the issue of Socialist members.

2

Moreover, the McNaboe investigation occurred at a time when the Democratic Party controlled the New York State Senate. Senator McNaboe, the committee chairman and by all odds the most extreme person connected with the investigation, was a New York City Democrat. Although the Coudert investigation was conducted by a Republican and drew most of its support from upstate Republicans, the resolution which led to its creation was introduced by a New York City Democrat, Senator Dunnigan.

The factors of party and city-upstate antagonism thus appear as elements although possibly not as direct causal factors in the readiness of the state legislature to probe into the institutions of New York City. Another factor which cuts across those already mentioned is that of religion. It would be an unwarranted magnifying of the facts to state that the Catholic Church was directly connected with these investigations; nevertheless, the influence of the church cannot be ignored. Catholic opposition had been chiefly instrumental in the nullification of the appointment of Bertrand Russell to the faculty of City College in 1940. In introducing his resolution calling for an investigation of the city schools, Senator Dunnigan was strongly influenced by what he regarded as "ungodly" conduct on the part of certain educational officials.

In the course of the investigation it was frequently alleged that the Roman Catholic Church was behind the inquiry and that the investigation was being used as a screen for attacking Jewish teachers. This statement has been repeated to the writer on several occasions, but no tangible evidence has been marshaled to support such a charge. Certain superficial facts existed: most of the persons named as Communists were Jewish; the chairman of the investigating committee and some members of his staff were Catholic. Other members of the committee staff were Jewish, however, and there is no satisfactory evidence to suggest any direct connection between

3

religious affiliation and the inquiry. The uncompromising antagonism between the Roman Catholic Church and communism is too well known to require comment. No one would expect the clergy or members of the faith to maintain an attitude of strict neutrality under such circumstances. More than this cannot be said.

Some observers have attempted to discover a connection between the composition of the New York State Legislature and the recurrent investigations. The hypothesis in this case builds upon the assumption that the caliber of New York legislative personnel is not high. In the absence of more persuasive evidence than now exists, this theory cannot be accorded serious weight. Criteria for appraising legislators are not available, so it is not possible to compare the New York product with that found in Pennsylvania, Massachusetts, California, or Minnesota. This inadequacy in our political science does not seem particularly serious. It seems doubtful that comparative statistics would help much because a legislator might be adequate in Ohio and unsatisfactory in Connecticut or North Carolina.

But New York legislators are a varied lot, and it seems likely that the range from mediocrity to excellence does not greatly differ from that in any other state. Certainly men of character and high ability are to be found in every session. There has been wide disparity in the quality of legislative personnel actively engaged in such investigations, and this disparity has been readily reflected in the quality of the inquiry itself. But other than this rather obvious comment no other generalization seems justified.

The materials that follow do not furnish a ready answer to the question of why New York has achieved the dubious distinction of adding to its numerous firsts in so many fields that of having had more loyalty investigations than any other state, unless, possibly, these two things go together. Certainly the ferment of opinion, prejudice, and discontent is always high in New York. The extremes of old and new, rich and poor, radicalism and reaction all find fertile surroundings in this crossroads of humanity. It is under conditions such as these that tensions mount and demand response. Legislative bodies in New York are not radical in composition and sentiment. In general, they tend to be dominated by rural rather than by urban representatives—persons not especially sympathetic to the problems which urban conditions aggravate nor to the groups which attempt to find solutions.

The emphasis in the following study, which spans a period of approximately thirty years, is upon the action of the New York State Legislature concerning acts of disloyalty on the part of individuals and groups. A legislature does not function in a political or social vacuum, however. Any action taken by the legislature or a committee of that body usually grows out of some problem in the society of which the legislature is but a part. Moreover, the action of the legislature does not terminate the investigation. The Rapp-Coudert committee concluded its work in 1940 but in its wake there followed a series of investigations, trials, and dismissals by the Board of Higher Education of New York City.

This phase of the search for subversives in the New York educational system was not legislative and therefore strictly speaking does not fall within the scope of a survey of legislative activity. In another sense, however, the resolutions, investigations, and trials carried on by the Board of Higher Education were an integral part of the broad public inquiry of which the Rapp-Coudert investigation was merely an earlier phase. If there had been no legislative investigation, there would have been no subsequent action by the board. Its entry into the investigation was belated and reluctant.

At an earlier period the board had taken public notice of the charge that Communists were present among the student bodies and staffs of the city's schools. It had then taken the position that their presence was not a cause for concern or punitive action and had justified its stand on the ground that such groups merely reflected a healthy diversity of opinion to be expected in a democratic society.

When the Rapp-Coudert committee first embarked upon its work, the Board of Higher Education retained its attitude of passive neutrality. Later, in response to a request from Senator Coudert, the board issued a mild resolution directing those within its jurisdiction to co-operate with the committee. Not until pointed expressions of dissatisfaction came from the committee chairman concerning the lack of board support did the board actually take an active part in the inquiry, although some members had urged a more vigorous course from the outset.

When the first group of alleged Communists on the teaching and administrative staffs was made public, the board's attitude changed. From that time the board itself became the focal point and assumed greater significance than the committee. The legislative investigation and the trials thus constitute integral parts of a single episode. One cannot analyze one phase without including the other because they overlap and intertwine so completely. Their roots are identical and their development and end product inseparable.

The materials for this study have been gathered from many sources. The records of the New York Legislature, including committee hearings and reports, have been basic references, but these official sources stop far short of supplying a complete account of the events they document. Supplementary material has been obtained from the files of the Board of Higher Education, the Teachers Union, and the American Civil Liberties Union. The transcripts of the legislative committee hearings and trials of teachers in the removal cases have proved some of the most valuable sources. Several persons who had no official connection with the Rapp-Coudert investigation but who were very close to it kept notes or files and were kind enough to make them available.

Newspaper files are indispensable for the leads they provide and the thread of continuity they supply, but they also tell only part of the story. Without them the researcher would be adrift upon a chartless sea, but an account reconstructed wholly from press reports inevitably presents a picture in which the bright and striking colors tend to blot out the more subdued shades which must be included if the reproduction is to depict fruitfully the original.

Many individuals have added their recollections. Among this group have been members of the investigating committee and its staff, members of the Board of Higher Education and its staff, members of the administrative and teaching staffs of the municipal schools and colleges, including several of those who faced charges and underwent trial and dismissal, officials, counsel, and members of the teachers' unions, and others who had no official connection with the investigation and trials but followed them carefully. Some of these individuals have talked freely; others have been reluctant to discuss events to which they were unwilling participants or witnesses. In some instances their co-operation was obtained only after full assurance that their identity would remain undisclosed. It should be added that not all who co-operated requested anonymity. Nevertheless, rather than include only a partial list of those interviewed, it has seemed preferable to omit all names. My debt to them is no less real for this omission.

Numerous instances occurred in which persons who were personally involved in some of the events discussed below gave conflicting versions of a particular incident. Situations of this kind present a dilemma which cannot always be resolved satisfactorily. It is difficult if not impossible to distill the full truth from such a welter of conflicting reports. In such instances where external checks by which contradictory claims might be reconciled were lacking, it has seemed safer and more prudent to omit the point entirely. Even with this policy of caution it has sometimes been necessary to draw conclusions that cannot be fully documented.

I

The Lusk Investigation

THE Lusk investigation did not suddenly appear upon a serene and untroubled scene. Labor unrest, a feature of any postwar readjustment, was especially aggravated in 1919 by the appearance or unprecedented growth of politico-economic radicalism among labor organizations. The Industrial Workers of the World preached and practiced a program that was militantly aggressive, and the program's appeal was demonstrated by the rapidity with which it swept through the country, gaining clamorous adherents as it went. Simultaneously, local activities—real or imagined—of agents of the Bolshevik government became a cause for great worry in certain circles.

The extremely articulate character of the radical groups coupled with highly colored rumors of violence produced a state of mind that bordered on hysteria. Much of the difficulty was traceable to the absence or unreliability of information. There was genuine need for a careful, judicious sifting of the facts. It was in this setting that the events leading to the creation of the Lusk committee occurred.

In the weeks immediately preceding the creation of the Lusk committee, a variety of episodes had revealed an increasing uneasiness on the part of certain public officials. In January, 1919, a teacher had been suspended from Commercial

High School, New York City, for the alleged utterance of Bolshevist doctrines in the classroom.[1] A few days later a person whose name was soon to be intimately linked with the Lusk investigation told a committee of the United States Senate that Soviets were then conducting propaganda schools for children and adults in all the largest cities of the country.[2] The Judiciary Committee of the United States Senate, already engaged in an investigation of subversive activities, was directed by a new resolution to institute a broad inquiry into all forms of anti-American radicalism.[3]

During the course of the next few weeks a subcommittee of of the Senate Judiciary Committee held a number of public hearings. Several witnesses who had recently returned from Europe told shocking tales of the brutality that had accompanied Soviet seizure of power in Russia. Much emphasis was placed upon the important roles being played in the revolution by persons who had formerly lived in the United States, especially East Side New York.[4] Solicitor General W. H. Lamar informed the subcommittee of a plot to overthrow the government and expressed apprehension over the large number of English and foreign language papers that were being published by the IWW.

On March 12, the police raided the headquarters of the Union of Russian Peasant Workers of America in New York, arrested two hundred persons, and seized quantities of radical literature. The following day criminal charges were lodged against four persons as the district attorney's office announced that their well-financed organization swore its members to violence and destruction of property.[5]

By the time the resolution creating the New York legislative committee had been approved in March, 1919, the pattern

1 *New York Times,* January 19, 1919, p. 4.
2 *Ibid.,* January 22, 1919, p. 3. 4 *Ibid.,* February 13, 14, 1919, pp. 1, 2.
3 *Ibid.,* February 5, 1919, p. 1. 5 *Ibid.,* March 14, 1919, p. 8.

of its findings had already been well forecast by what had occurred during the preceding months. The public had been regaled with tales of violence abroad and alleged conspiracy at home. Ominous threats of widespread networks of radical organizations poised for attack were supplemented by claims that propaganda campaigns and school infiltration were being employed to undermine American institutions. These were the charges which gave birth to the inquiry. They were likewise the charges which emanated from the inquiry. The investigation presented numerous variations on this theme; it did little more.

Clayton Lusk, a lawyer from Cortland, New York, was named chairman. Senator Lusk had been a member of the legislature only since January. The reasons for his selection for this post have never been made clear. He continued to serve in the Senate until 1924 where he subsequently enjoyed some prominence. He filled the posts of president pro tem and majority leader in 1921 and minority leader in 1923. In 1922 he served briefly as acting lieutenant governor and acting governor.

Late in March, 1919, shortly after the resolution creating the committee had been approved but before the staff had been selected, Senator Lusk held several conferences with Attorney-General Charles D. Newton. From these sessions came the decision not to engage special counsel for the committee. Instead, the Attorney-General himself was designated to fill this post.

Information available does not reveal the considerations that led Senator Lusk and his colleagues of the legislature to utilize Attorney-General Newton as committee counsel. Finances may have been a factor, because the allowance for the committee had been reduced from $50,000 to $30,000 when the Senate resolution reached the Assembly. An equally plausible reason may have been found in the Attorney-General himself. He was singularly active during the organizational stages of the investigation, and his prominent role during the inquiry suggests that he personally may have been chiefly instrumental in persuading the committee to utilize the facilities of his office.

The Lusk committee was organized in May and began to collect materials. At the suggestion of Attorney-General Newton, Chairman Lusk organized a secret-service force to gather information. A staff of translators was also engaged to examine foreign-language newspapers, periodicals, and pamphlets. The committee had its first big news break on June 12, when its operatives raided the headquarters of the Russian Soviet Bureau in New York City. It held its first public hearing on the same day.

The committee continued to conduct raids and hold public hearings throughout the remainder of 1919 and into 1920. Most of the activity took place in New York City, although in December activities were transferred temporarily to upstate New York, where the usual procedure of a raid followed by a public hearing was employed in Buffalo, Utica, and Rochester. Early in January, 1920, the committee returned to New York City, where it conducted another series of raids, this time of the headquarters of radical publications. A final series of public hearings at which the witnesses were leading educators completed the inquiry. In March the committee issued a preliminary report which included several legislative proposals. With its final report, dated April 24, 1920, the Lusk committee terminated its existence just a few weeks more than a year after it had been established.

It is impossible to judge any investigation by its financial record. A well-conducted legislative inquiry into some aspect of public policy or governmental administration frequently contributes heavily to the public interest, yet such values cannot be computed in dollars and cents. In the case of the Lusk committee, however, the financial record is hopelessly confused. The committee started out with its initial appropriation of $30,000. Although it did not directly receive additional public funds, financial assistance was obtained in other ways. It was announced on January 29, 1920, that the committee's total expenditures had been $80,000.[6] The additional $50,000 had been advanced to the committee, $10,000 at a time, by State Comptroller Travis as a private loan from an Albany bank. Mr. Travis stated that he assumed personal responsibility for the arrangement. This announcement was made two months before the committee report went to press, so it may be assumed that additional funds were found to cover the cost of publishing the four heavy volumes totaling more than four thousand pages.

The financial ramifications of the Lusk committee extend much beyond the funds already mentioned, however. Through its operating relationship with the State Attorney-General's office, the local prosecuting attorneys, and the state and local police forces, not to mention occasional collaboration from the United States Department of Justice and the Immigration Service, the committee was able to utilize official personnel far beyond that on its own payroll. On some of its raids it employed more than seven hundred uniformed police. When to this figure are added the various specialized plain-clothes corps, the committee was actually functioning with a staff of over a thousand persons. Included in the total were a number of private detectives employed from time to time. Presumably they were engaged and compensated by the committee, although this point is not clear because no official accounting of its expenditures was ever made.

6 *Ibid.*, January 30, 1920, p. 3.

The Lusk Committee's Conception of Its Function

The methods employed by the Lusk committee were more extreme than those of any other legislative investigating agency that has come to the attention of this writer. At least part of the explanation for its arbitrary procedures may be traced to its failure to comprehend the nature of the legislative investigative function and to distinguish it from that of agencies charged with law enforcement. In actual operation this distinction was never made. The chairman of the committee either did not recognize or chose to ignore the danger of merging two unrelated functions. In his first public statement explaining the committee's objectives, he revealed a conception of its function much broader than that of eliciting information:

It seems to me that the committee should at its first hearings find out, and the public generally know, just what these radicals are advocating and just what they propose to accomplish. If the movement is simply political, if this radical effort is simply political, if this radical effort is simply for the purpose of lawfully bringing about a greater measure of justice to the working class, then the work of this committee is at an end except insofar as this committee can cooperate with them in enacting legislation to bring about these results. If, on the other hand, this movement is seditious, if it aims at the unlawful, violent, and forcible overthrow of our institutions, if its purpose is to violently destroy the Constitution and legal protection to personal liberties, then the committee will make such further investigation *and take such action, both preventive and constructive, as seems necessary for the protection of our institutions and the persons and property of the citizens of the state.*

If the latter situation is found to exist, we shall ask for, and have already been assured, the full cooperation of the state and city police. We shall ask for and expect the full cooperation of the different departments of the state, county, and city governments, and of the Federal investigating bureaus. The committee is bi-partisan. Its work will be carried on with an absolutely open mind and without regard to politics and personalities and solely with the view of ascertaining the facts and *affording such protection to the people of the state as seems necessary in view of such disclosures as the investigation brings forth.*[7]

This language seems strange as a description of the task of a legislative investigating committee. That it was not merely carelessness in terminology was borne out by subsequent developments. Not only do the actions of the committee—to be described later—partake largely of the police function; the public statements released by the committee's chairman or by its counsel leave no room for doubt. Some representative examples are included for purposes of illustration. On July 12, after the raids on the Russian Soviet Bureau and various local organizations, including the Rand School and the headquarters of the left-wing Socialists, a spokesman for the committee stated that most of the evidence gathered by its investigators would not be made public.[8] He explained that, although the committee had twenty secret investigators at work, their findings were to be used as a basis for prosecution, hence would not be disclosed. This bears closer resemblance to a function of the police than of a legislative investigating committee.

When a Cleveland lawyer, who had been in Russia during the period of violent revolution, appeared before the committee, he declared that a woman who had been one of the leading figures in the movement had since come to New York. Associate Counsel Stevenson immediately set some of the committee's special agents upon her trail.[9] The incident was never referred to again, but it afforded the committee another opportunity to dramatize itself as a police agency. This impression was fortified by the long secret conference which the

[7] *Ibid.,* June 4, 1919, p. 3. Italics added.
[8] *Ibid.,* July 13, 1919, p. 16.   [9] *Ibid.,* July 26, 1919, p. 5.

committee announced had been held among Chairman Lusk, Attorney-General Newton (committee counsel), Assistant District Attorney Alexander I. Rorke, assigned to the committee, and Special Agent A. B. Schnell of the deportation division of the United States Immigration Service. Senator Lusk declined to disclose what took place at this important meeting, but his comment a couple of weeks later helps to round out the picture. After the abortive Rand School trial, the committee decided to postpone further hearings. In making this announcement, Senator Lusk explained that during the month of August the employees of the committee would be assisting District Attorney Swann in preparing and prosecuting seditious activity cases before the Supreme Court, in preparing the new case against the Rand School, and in assisting the Federal Departments of Justice and Labor prepare cases against undesirable aliens held for deportation. An odd statement from the chairman of a legislative investigating committee.[10]

On November 8, 1919, the committee conducted sweeping raids upon seventy-odd so-called "Red Centers" in New York City. More than one thousand persons were taken into custody and tons of literature were seized. Senator Lusk explained his committee's action:

It is the plain statement of the intention of members of this organization [Communist Party] to overthrow our established government by force and unlawful means. . . . These organizations are a direct public challenge to the authorities of the State and nation. . . . It seems to me that the time has come to put into force stern measures to do away with this agitation and punish these disloyal leaders in the movement.[11]

Mr. Lusk was not speaking as one recommending new legislation but as an adjunct of the executive machinery.

An even more clear-cut example of the committee's concep-

10 *Ibid.*, July 31, 1919, p. 15.   11 *Ibid.*, November 9, 1919, p. 1.

tion of itself as an agency of law enforcement occurred during the last weeks of its existence. On January 3, 1920, Associate Counsel Stevenson and the New York City police raided the offices of four radical publications. Deputy Attorney-General Berger, committee counsel, explained, "The entire current issue of the four papers seized was more than 10,000 pounds. . . . The estimated cost of the production of the printing seized is substantially more than $20,000. . . . The important part of these raids is that they struck at the source of radical propaganda." [12]

Senator Lusk's comment revealed the same point of view: "The raids in this city on Saturday night on the radical newspapers, *The Communist World, Der Kampf,* and *Robitnick,* struck at the very fountain head of Communism." [13] This sounds more like the axe and sledge hammer of the constabulary than the searchlight of the legislative committee.

The Armed Raid as an Instrument of Legislative Power

In the preceding paragraphs official statements of the committee chairman and members of his staff have been reproduced for the purpose of presenting the committee's own conception of its job. The record of events provides a much fuller and more eloquent account. What the committee did is of greater significance than what it said. Attention will now be shifted to this phase.

First of all, whereas the normal instrumentality of an investigating committee is the public or private hearing implemented by the subpoena and *subpoena duces tecum,* the Lusk committee employed the search warrant, chiefly the John Doe variety. The committee was authorized to issue subpoenas and in some instances it did make use of this power, but the search warrant was a much more dramatic weapon and the committee apparently could not resist its use even when the less spectac-

[12] *Ibid.,* January 5, 1920, p. 2.   [13] *Ibid.,* January 7, 1920, p. 1.

ular subpoena would have been equally effective in turning up the information sought.

In its first foray, the committee singled out the headquarters of the "Representative in the United States of America of the Russian Socialist Federal Soviet Republic," popularly known as the Russian Soviet Bureau and the Soviet Mission, located at 110 West 40th Street. The raid was conducted by state troopers and private detectives on the authority of a sweeping search warrant issued by City Magistrate Alexander Brough.

The raiding party descended upon the unsuspecting Soviet representative and his staff, took them into custody, refusing to let them consult legal counsel, cut the telephone wires and literally cleaned out the offices. All papers were removed, including a file marked diplomatic correspondence. The bank accounts of the mission and the private accounts of individuals were seized along with hundreds of books, pamphlets, and miscellaneous literature. The members of the mission, including Ludwig C. A. K. Martens, Soviet Representative, were taken under police guard to the City Hall, where the committee was in public session, and there subjected to a three-hour grilling.

Mr. Martens was the official representative of the Soviet government then in power in Russia. He had credentials to substantiate his claim and he immediately protested the legality of the committee's action against him. The committee steadfastly ignored his appeals, justifying its position by calling him the "so-called Soviet Representative," although it took great pains to establish the fact that he was in constant communication with the Soviet government and received financial support from it.

At this time the State Department in Washington, uncertain as to the ultimate outcome of the revolution, civil war, and international conquest then being waged within Russia, was reluctant to show its hand. It had simply failed to respond to Martens' repeated efforts to establish official relations. His position was an anomalous one, but he had been able to establish the validity of his claims sufficiently to persuade such practical concerns as the Ford Motor Company and Swift and Company to contract with him for business with his government.

It might be assumed that a state agency would under such circumstances give at least some consideration to the delicate issues that might arise from its invasion of the international arena. But the committee was no respecter of amenities whether international or domestic. Several aspects of this incident are worthy of comment.

Apparently Senator Lusk was somewhat apprehensive of the heavy-handed methods employed in this first raid. When questioned by the press, he disclaimed all knowledge of the use of search warrants. He explained that he had issued a *subpoena duces tecum* for five members of the Soviet Mission and added that his questioners would have to consult Attorney-General Newton about any search warrant. He accounted for the presence of state troopers with the explanation that the committee was using them as process servers. The chairman managed to convey the impression that he knew but wasn't telling by his concluding observation, which he was reported to have made with a smile: "It seems that by some strange coincidence some other proceeding affecting the Soviet Mission is under way at the very moment our committee want the members of the mission as witnesses; such things happen once in a while." [14] Although the Senator spoke in jest, his statement that "some other proceeding affecting the Soviet Mission is under way" was ironically true, for in effect the Lusk committee was functioning simultaneously as a fact-finding arm of the legislature and as a search and seizure agency of the executive.

[14] *Ibid.,* June 13, 1919, p. 1.

Attorney-General Newton also denied any connection with the search warrants. His statement to the press, "I understand that Archibald E. Stevenson, Secretary of the Union League Club, got some officer to swear to the information upon which the search warrant was issued," [15] was plainly not uttered in good faith. It turned out that Stevenson had been appointed associate counsel to the Lusk committee. Either Mr. Newton was co-operating with private individuals clothed neither with authority nor responsibility or he was in the uncomplimentary position of permitting his subordinates to engage in arbitrary activities—whether with or without his knowledge is not clear. The entire incident of the use of search warrants to further the objectives of a legislative investigating committee casts doubt upon the good intentions and sound judgment of those responsible.

After executing the search warrant and taking possession of everything except the office furniture, the raiders made off with their booty. But instead of delivering the seized documents to the magistrate for his determination as to their disposition, the committee's agents took them to its own headquarters. Not until almost a week later, when suit was brought to vacate the warrant, was the committee's arrogant disregard of the legal requirements and the judicial officers' negligence fully revealed. Not only had the committee resorted to arbitrary procedures in obtaining its information, but it had also disregarded the law in its application of these extreme powers, and it had entered into collusion with another branch of the government to do so.

Throughout its existence the Lusk committee continued to employ the raid as its chief instrumentality. On June 21, simultaneous raids were made upon the Rand School of Social Science, the "Russian Branch" of the Industrial Workers of

[15] *Ibid.*

20

the World, and the headquarters of the left-wing Socialists.[16] As before, the search warrants were extremely general and the raiders carried off virtually everything that could be moved.[17] In the case of the Rand School fifty persons took part and trucks were still busy carting away the "evidence" several hours later. Not content with its first haul, the committee

[16] The Rand School of Social Science, which was to bear the brunt of the Lusk committee's attacks, deserves brief comment. Founded in 1906 from the proceeds of a trust fund in the will of the late Carrie D. Rand, the school was established as the educational branch of the Labor and Socialist movement. Throughout its existence, down to the present day, the Rand School has distinguished sharply between peaceful socialism, which it has always espoused, and totalitarian doctrines, to which it has always been opposed. In 1919–1920, as well as at the present time, the school has been recognized and welcomed by civic leaders as a constructive agency in the field of workers' education and research. In addition to daytime and evening classes, the Rand School continues to operate a library and bookstore at its present address of 7 East 15th Street, New York, New York.

[17] The sweeping nature of the search warrants issued to the Lusk committee is illustrated by the first warrant issued against the Rand School: "County of New York, In the name of the people of the State of New York. To any officer of the County of New York.

"Proof by affidavit having been this day made before me by Clarence L. Converse that certain books, papers, documents, printed, typed, and written, and other printed matters are in the possession of the Rand School of Social Science, the American Soviet Socialist Party, the Workers' World, and John Doe, Richard Roe, Thomas Poe, and Mary Roe, the said names being fictitious, true names unknown, but the persons so designated being the persons in charge . . . and that the foregoing [organizations and individuals] have used the same and intend to use the same as the means of committing a public offense against the laws of the State of New York and of bringing about the overthrow of organized government by force, violence, and unlawful means and of inciting riot and inciting the endangering of life and destruction of valuable property, you are therefore commanded at any time of the day or night or on Sunday to make immediate search of the premises specified in said affidavit for the following property.

"All publications, documents, books, circulars, letters, typed or printed matter having to do with anarchists, Socialists advocating violence, revolution, or Bolshevist activity, and all books, letters, papers pertaining to the action or business carried on in said offices, and all circulars and literature of any sort,

21

agents returned two days later with a new warrant, forcibly opened the safe, and made off with all of its contents.

On November 9 occurred the prize raid of all. Aided by approximately one thousand assorted federal, state, and local officials, the committee's agents swooped down upon seventy-three "Red Centers" in New York City.[18] The customary procedure—seizure of all papers, records, and publications—more than twenty-five tons of it—was supplemented in this case by the arrest of all persons found on the premises. Almost a thousand "radicals" were caught up in the net and hustled off to jail. After some preliminary questioning, thirty-five were detained without bail; the rest were permitted to leave. Of those detained a half dozen were later convicted under the New York criminal anarchy law; a few were deported; the great majority were ultimately freed because of the lack of evidence against them.

In late December a series of upstate raids followed the now familiar pattern.[19] "Radical" propaganda was impounded; "dangerous revolutionaries" were taken into custody, most of them to be turned loose subsequently without the filing of any charges against them. For its final foray the committee returned to New York City. This time it cleaned out and confiscated the entire current editions of four "radical" publications.[20] If any additional evidence is needed to prove that the committee did not conceive its function to be the limited one of eliciting information, it is supplied abundantly in the statement of the committee counsel, Deputy Attorney-General Samuel A. Berger:

---

kind, or character, and if you find the same or any part thereof, to bring it forthwith before me at the Magistrate's Court, 300 Mulberry Street, New York. William McAdoo, Chief City Magistrate of the City of New York. Dated at 300 Mulberry Street, June 21, 1919."

[18] *New York Times,* November 9, 10, 1919, p. 1.

[19] *Ibid.,* December 31, 1919, p. 19; January 1, 1920, p. 17.

[20] *Ibid.,* January 4, 5, 1920, pp. 1, 2.

The entire current issue of the four papers seized was more than ten thousand pounds. In addition, the books, cards, records, and mailing lists, as well as the type from which the mailing lists and newspapers were printed, were also seized, also large quantities of printed and bound books of a revolutionary nature. The estimated cost of the production of the printing seized is substantially more than $20,000.

The important part of these raids is that they struck at the source of radical propaganda. We also took a large quantity of Lenin's letter to the American workingmen. . . . The most important thing found in the raids last night was the place where "Khlieb Y Dolya" which translates means "Bread and Freedom," was printed. . . . We also took in the raids two excellent oil paintings—one of Lenin and the other of Trotsky.[21]

From first to last the Lusk committee abused its use of the search warrant by failing to specify in particularity what it was looking for or to furnish concrete evidence that the objects sought were being used as instrumentalities of law violation. The committee must bear responsibility for initiating this illegal precedure, but the plan would have failed had not the magistrate's courts supplied generous collaboration. Chief Magistrate William M. McAdoo set an example that his colleagues would find difficult to exceed. Upon flimsy evidence he issued blanket search warrants which authorized indiscriminate seizure of everything in sight. He permitted committee agents to take full possession of the seized matter until counsel for the organizations raided forced him to honor the legal restrictions applicable. When the arrests were made, thirty-five persons charged with being members of the Communist Party were held. When they applied to Chief Magistrate McAdoo for a reduction of bail, he ruled that inasmuch as the Communist Party intended to destroy organized government,

[21] *Ibid.*

every member of the party was guilty. Accordingly, none of these held was entitled to have his bail reduced.

The only instance of even a faint and temporary gesture in the direction of more orderly procedure came about as a result of outside intercession. After the first raid, the Soviet Mission sought through counsel to vacate the search warrant on the dual grounds that it had been too general and had been illegally executed because the matter seized had not been returned to the tribunal issuing the warrant. After some delay the magistrate who had issued the warrant rejected these claims and the plaintiff announced his intention to appeal. The committee thereupon returned a considerable portion of the materials seized so the appeal was not pressed.

When the Rand School raid occurred, the same situation was presented, as the committee transferred the several truck loads of material directly to its own headquarters. The committee did take the trouble a couple of days later to report to the press that its staff was cataloguing the seizure so as to make a return to the magistrate, but within four days' time much Rand School data was put into the record through the public hearings before a return had ever been made. In fact, it was not until three weeks later that Chief Magistrate McAdoo, who had signed the search warrant, moved to act, and then only after he had been severely called to account by Samuel Untermyer, who volunteered his legal services on behalf of the school. The materials were temporarily turned over to the magistrate's court, but before long they were once again in the committee's possession.[22]

The Lusk Committee's Hearing Procedures

Besides the raid, the Lusk committee regularly employed the public hearing as an instrument of investigation. Perhaps

[22] Senator Lusk explained that he had subpoenaed the documents from Chief Magistrate McAdoo.

323.4 C3553y

C. 1

the term "public hearing" needs further amplification because as employed by the Lusk committee it took a rather special form. At no time was the general public admitted. Committee practice distinguished private and public hearings by admitting to the latter accredited members of the press. Ordinarily a public hearing which might run into several sessions was held shortly after a raid. The consistency with which these two steps followed in regular juxtaposition suggests that the heightened dramatic effect of the public hearing was a product consciously sought. After each raid the chairman or counsel would open the subsequent hearing with a rather extended commentary upon the significance of the raid, the nature and extent of the material seized, and the advantages accruing from it. Neither Senator Lusk nor his counsel exercised conspicuous restraint in these reports. Invariably one encounters claims which later committee revelations fail to produce. The impression prevails that the psychology of the side-show barker dominated these "reporting" sessions.

The succeeding public sessions of the committee would be occupied chiefly by its counsel or agents who would read into the record various documents, letters, speeches, and publications. The purpose was ostensibly that of constructing from official sources an accurate picture of the nature and extent of the organized effort to overthrow the government. An examination of the materials introduced during the public hearings shows a much less complimentary picture of what actually took place. There is not even a semblance of any effort to present an orderly, comprehensive account of the extent of radical organization and action. Instead, the hearing provided a platform from which miscellaneous articles could be put on display for the sensational responses they might produce. Items were read into the record for the purpose of creating particular impressions. If misrepresentation was necessary to accomplish this result, the committee chairman or counsel did not

25

hesitate to indulge. If the aim shifted from time to time, it occasioned the committee no embarrassment to shift its ground accordingly and cite the same data to prove another case.

These are serious charges, but they grow directly out of the record. Some representative examples are presented. On June 27, following the raid on the Rand School, Associate Counsel Archibald Stevenson read into the record what Senator Lusk called the most important evidence yet turned up by his committee. The document in question was described as a propaganda plan for organizing southern Negroes. The manuscript had been found in one of the desks at the Rand School. There was no trace of evidence that the school had any connection with the manuscript and certainly no indication that the "plan" had ever progressed beyond the writing stage. Deputy Attorney-General Samuel A. Berger, committee counsel, identified the author of the manuscript as W. A. Domingo, a Negro lecturer and writer. Although it was implied that he had some official connection with the Rand School, the relationship was never made clear. Nor was evidence introduced to show that definite action had been taken to carry the plans into effect. Furthermore, the document itself was completely innocuous. The article took the general line that the Negro had been race-conscious but not class-conscious. The task of the Socialists was to transmute race consciousness into class consciousness. Concrete suggestions were offered on such practical points as what methods of appeal would be most effective.

As Mr. Berger read the entire article to the committee, he stressed particularly the specific steps or methods that were recommended for achieving the plan's objectives. In view of the obvious horror with which he and the committee received these suggestions, they are of special interest for the light they throw upon the committee's conception of seditious activity. Mr. Domingo's recommendations—directed at the Socialist Party—were incorporated in nine proposals:

1. Condemn all acts of injustice to the Negro.

2. Socialists must stress lynchings in the South and condemn them.

3. Give Negroes more prominence in the discussion; they like that.

4. Do everything to attract Negroes to our meetings. Report and denounce all cases of racial discrimination that come to our knowledge, especially by the labor unions.

5. Launch a special proposal among Negroes to show them the benefits they will derive from the economic changes we propose.

6. Subsidize radical Negro newspapers.

7. Send radical white speakers to spread radical propaganda among the Negroes, especially in the South, where the black hosts are most likely to organize into a "mercenary army." Show them "the shame of our democracy" by emphasizing the discrimination practiced in elections. Show them that Christ, Wm. Lloyd Garrison, the Abolitionist, and Abraham Lincoln were denounced as radicals in their day, while today they are regarded as great benefactors of the race.

8. Induce intelligent Negroes to attend radical meetings of the whites and impress upon them that the Socialists are their friends.

9. Avoid stressing problems of race and emphasize the advantages to all of the cooperative commonwealth.

Nothing in the entire document suggested violence. In fact, the tenor of the entire communication was wholly that of peaceful, evolutionary socialism.

The plain purpose of the committee in introducing this document was (1) to create the impression that the Rand School was actively engaged in implementing a conspiratorial plan of action and (2) to create the belief that the plan in question involved violence. In Senator Lusk's own words, he regarded "this evidence of a detailed plan for the spreading of Bolshevist propaganda among Negroes of the South as the greatest menace the evidence before the committee so far has

27

disclosed." [23] If this statement represents an honest conviction, Senator Lusk was ill-equipped to conduct such an inquiry.

On another occasion when correspondence from the files of the Soviet Bureau was being put into the record, Mr. Stevenson read from a memorandum by Evans Clark, associate director of the commercial department of the Soviet Bureau, reporting that he had talked with Dudley Field Malone, Amos Pinchot, Judah Magnes, Gilbert E. Roe, and Lincoln Colcord regarding the desire of manufacturers to export their products, etc., "and other matters of concern to the bureau." To a query from Senator Lusk if there was anything to indicate what these "other matters" were, Mr. Stevenson replied:

> Not a thing, but it might be interesting to note that Dudley Field Malone was one of the speakers at the Madison Square Garden protest against the action of your committee, that Amos Pinchot and Judah Magnes have been active in various pacifist organizations, and that Lincoln Colcord, I believe but am not sure, is with the *Nation*.[24]

Sensational Publicity: The Technique of Smear

The tendency to stamp as subversive any activity or expression to which the committee took exception—whether it was pacifism, liberalism, or just honest disagreement with the purposes and methods of the committee—crops up repeatedly throughout the investigation. This lack of discrimination is the more reprehensible because of the committee's habitual practice of dragging in the names of persons upon the least pretext. The technique of smear by slanting innuendo runs through almost every public statement. Many examples could be cited, but a single one will serve.

Among the items read into the public record from the files of the Soviet Bureau were selected names found on a mailing list. Especial care was taken to draw attention to such persons

[23] *New York Times,* June 28, 1919, pp. 1, 3.
[24] *Ibid.,* June 27, 1919, p. 2.

as Paul U. Kellogg, editor of *Survey,* Dean George W. Kirch-
wey of Columbia Law School, Professor Carlton J. H. Hayes,
and others.[25] In a letter to the *New York Times,* Mr. Kellogg
protested the unfair tactic. Part of the letter is reproduced because it shows how unjustified such disclosures were and what
misrepresentation could result:

If the committee had seen fit to raid the anti-Bolshevist officials
of the Russian Information Bureau, it would have probably found
my name on the mailing list of that organization too. The *Survey*
is anxious to have all the press matter and fugitive literature that
is going.

The ostensible purpose of Mr. Stevenson in publishing this
mailing list was to show that the Soviet Bureau was acting outside
its ostensible commercial purpose and engaging in propaganda.
But I gather that this list is lugged in rather to daub some perfectly
good names. It tends to discredit the liberals whose names are
included: discomfit them in their work, discount among people
who are unacquainted with the circumstances, any stand they
may take in the future.[26]

At the first public hearing following the raid on the Soviet
Mission, Archibald Stevenson, associate counsel, spent the entire day reading into the record documents and letters from
the Mission's files to show that Martens and his organization
had received large sums of money from Russia and that while
he claimed that his concern was chiefly that of negotiating
commercial agreements with American business firms, he was
actually dealing mostly with radicals and agitators.[27] A few
days later Mr. Stevenson appeared again, this time to present
evidence to show that the Soviet Bureau had been negotiating
with 1,500 American business concerns—a point directly contrary to the statement he had made just a few days before. The
strong implication was that the firms named were guilty of
disloyalty by negotiating with Soviet representatives.[28]

[25] *Ibid.,* June 20, 1919, p. 1. [27] *Ibid.,* June 13, 1919, p. 1.
[26] *Ibid.,* June 22, 1919, p. 1. [28] *Ibid.,* June 27, 1919, p. 2.

In addition to the press fodder provided by the public hearings, the committee through chairman or counsel turned out a steady stream of publicity. Almost daily press conferences were supplemented by frequent press releases or formal public statements. Honors were about evenly distributed between Senator Lusk and Attorney-General Newton, although Deputy Attorney-General Berger was not badly outdistanced. The same technique of sly insinuation, misleading half-truths, and disingenuous interpretations show that the public hearing and the press conference were all of a piece.

Random examples of a practice that was employed regularly demonstrate the reckless character of the committee's public statements. On July 20 the committee announced it had documentary evidence that the IWW were organizing American marine workers because they had a working agreement with the marine workers in many foreign countries to paralyze industry in pursuance of the slogan: "When transportation stops, industry stops." [29] Like so many other sensational claims emanating from the committee only to be dropped for an even more sensational one the following day, the committee never followed this one up.

Two days later the committee captured headlines with a report from one of its secret operatives that a plan was afoot to organize a "Red Guard" in the United States to function as an adjunct of the Red Terror in Russia.[30] This flaming rumor was never revived, but a couple of days later the committee announced dramatically that its agents were combing the city for a mysterious woman who was supposed to be a trusted lieutenant of Lenin and Trotsky.[31] The woman, Sarah Naumovna Rauvich, was shadowed in the press for a couple of days and then dropped for an even more sensational claim. Deputy Attorney-General Berger disclosed his discovery that

[29] *Ibid.*, July 21, 1919, p. 6.   [31] *Ibid.*, July 26, 1919, p. 5.
[30] *Ibid.*, July 23, 1919, p. 28.

the Red press in New York City was being financed by rich radicals. He did not identify the culprits; the subject was dropped.[32]

The committee seemed to find particular pleasure in implicating prominent persons or institutions no matter how shoddy or ill-founded its information. On December 26, one of its investigators testified that Bakunin's *God and the State,* translated into English by the American anarchist, Benjamin R. Tucker, was in the New York Public Library. The investigator also disclosed that Mr. Anderson, the librarian, had written the Union of Russian Workers for issues of their revolutionary paper, *Bread and Freedom,* copies of which were now in the library.[33] It is clear from the context of the statement that the action of the librarian had raised the committee's suspicions.

A few days later the scapegoat was the Amalgamated Clothing Workers' Union. After committee hearings in Utica and Rochester, Senator Lusk declared that there was a close connection between strikes in the garment industry and the Communist Party. While it was explained that much of the evidence could not be divulged, the Amalgamated was linked in some mysterious way with the Rand School and Mr. Martens of the Soviet Bureau.[34] Mr. Lusk never troubled to amplify either his evidence or his sources of information concerning the union, nor did he see fit to acknowledge the inaccuracy of his statement when he was informed that the Amalgamated Clothing Workers' Union was the only organization which had made strikes illegal. The Senator merely shifted his attack, for within a week he was quoted in a full-dress interview:

More than 20,000 alien enemies in the Communist Party of New York State alone are openly organized for the overthrow of the

32 *Ibid.,* July 29, 1919, p. 6. 34 *Ibid.,* January 2, 3, 1920, p. 2.
33 *Ibid.,* December 27, 1919, p. 23.

Government by force and violence under the direction of Bolshevist leaders in Russia. In addition to these, there are the Communist Labor Party and other revolutionary organizations working actively to accomplish the same ends.

He went on to declare that evidence had been obtained proving that the propagandists were subverting even Sunday schools as channels for radicalism.[35]

The Rand School Episode

Perhaps no other single incident shows quite so clearly the committee's tendency to make claims without substantial factual proof as its ill-starred effort to revoke the charter of the Rand School of Social Science. A week after the raid, Attorney-General Newton stated that an examination of its files provided incontrovertible evidence that the school was engaged in plotting and preparing for violent seizure of the government. He announced his intention to move for immediate closing of the school and subsequent revocation of its charter. The headline of the *New York Times* reflects the tenor of Mr. Newton's press conference: "Moves to Close the Rand School; Attorney General Takes Steps toward Revoking Radical Institution's Charter; Planned Negro Uprising." [36]

In this instance the committee overreached itself. Many people who were not sympathetic to the Socialist Party were moved to protest against what appeared to be such extreme measures. Samuel Untermyer volunteered to serve as counsel for the school, whereupon the chairman of the committee made a characteristic statement: "That the Rand School had been able to retain a counsel of Mr. Untermyer's distinction has gone a long way to convince members of the Lusk committee that they were correct in their contention that the Rand School had powerful financial backing from sources yet un-

[35] *Ibid.*, January 7, 1920, p. 1.   [36] *Ibid.*, June 29, 1919, p. 1.

known to the public." [37] It was public knowledge that Mr. Untermyer was donating his services, but Senator Lusk could not resist the opportunity to twist the facts so as to create the opposite impression.

After trying his revocation action in the headlines for a few days, the Attorney-General suddenly changed his mind. Despite the insistence of Mr. Untermyer and of Supreme Court Justice McAvoy (in whose court the action had been taken) that the case be argued, Mr. Newton now sought several months' delay. He had hoped to close the school peremptorily by enjoining it from continuing to hold classes and operate its publishing business. He was not in a position to fight the case on its merits, so when Justice McAvoy declined to grant his petition for a temporary injunction until the case had been argued, he reluctantly agreed that the case should be tried within two weeks. A date was set and a special term of the Supreme Court ordered. Justice McAvoy enjoined both parties from discussing the case pending its presentation in court, but in less than a week Mr. Newton informed the press that he had found new evidence that the Rand School was fostering revolutionary teachings.[38]

Despite his new discoveries the Attorney-General showed no inclination to try his case in court. After invoking several unsuccessful devices to obtain a postponement, he was finally forced to admit that he was not ready to present his case. On the day set for trial Deputy Attorney-General Berger moved for postponement on the ground that Mr. Newton wanted to amend his complaint by incorporating new evidence. He explained that the Attorney-General wanted to examine the officers of the American Socialist Society, the parent organization of the Rand School, and to set up a commission to examine witnesses outside the state.

Both the opposing counsel and the court indicated their

[37] *Ibid.,* July 10, 1919, pp. 1, 4.   [38] *Ibid.,* July 17, 1919, p. 17.

willingness to accept oral amendments and even a week's postponement, but the Attorney-General pleaded that this was not enough. There was nothing to do under these circumstances except dismiss the case. Upon Mr. Untermyer's motion this was done, and the sensational Rand School case, which had begun with such blazing headlines, ended in a complete fizzle.[39]

The comment of Mr. Untermyer, although not that of a disinterested observer, is pertinent because it describes accurately the singular action of the committee counsel.

The outcome is the logical outgrowth of this scandalous suit. It was apparent from the day the action was begun that the Attorney General never intended to try it, and no matter how many actions he may begin, in my judgment he will never try them. Whether he eventually will disrupt the school and destroy freedom of speech and personal liberty remains to be seen.

Mr. Newton made a feeble attempt to save face. At the close of an executive session of the committee, he announced that he would renew his application to revoke the school's charter in the fall.[40] After a faint gesture to reopen the case in October, the matter was dropped altogether. No mention is made of this episode in the committee's final report.

The Lusk Committee Report

The final report of the Lusk committee, four thick volumes totaling more than four thousand pages, is a curious compilation of miscellaneous information. Well under 10 per cent of the total report is composed of original text from the committee itself. The remaining 90 per cent reproduces an indiscriminate assortment of literature upon a wide range of subjects. Documents illustrative of "Revolutionary and subversive movements at home and abroad" take up about half the re-

[39] *Ibid.*, July 31, 1919, p. 15.   [40] *Ibid.*

port. Of this material roughly a third is concerned with socialism in Europe. The rest deals documentarily not only with the several Socialist and Communist organizations active in the United States but also with anarchist and syndicalist movements and in addition "radical" labor unions, peace organizations, and agencies specializing in protecting civil liberties.

The report lumps together with no particular effort to distinguish their objectives, composition, or methods such diverse organizations as the Communist Party, the Amalgamated Clothing Workers, the Ford Peace Party, and the American Civil Liberties Union. The energy and enterprise of the committee in assembling so much data is counterbalanced by the crudeness of its attack.

The last two volumes are concerned with what the committee calls "constructive movements and measures in America." Approximately one fourth of the third volume treats such varied subjects as management-labor co-operation, the cooperative movement, the open-and-closed shop, compulsory arbitration, guild socialism, and the Plumb Plan. The remainder of Volume III and all of Volume IV reproduce materials which describe or illustrate citizenship training programs. Almost a thousand pages are taken up by detailed descriptions of the Americanization programs conducted by educational, religious, and social organizations in New York State. Volume IV reports information for the other forty-seven states on such topics as legislation on compulsory citizenship education, patriotic measures, display of flags, and instruction in the English language.

Senator Lusk explains the make-up of the final report in the following paragraphs:

The revolutionary movement being of an international character, involved and necessitated a study of conditions existing not

35

only in the State of New York but throughout the United States as well as in Europe and elsewhere: it is for that reason that this report necessarily is taken up, to a substantial extent, with a consideration of the conditions existing outside the State of New York.

. . .

The report is very largely made up of documents, the originals of which are in the possession of the committee. It has been the desire of the committee to eliminate personalities and put in only such evidence and documents as seemed absolutely necessary in order that a clear understanding might be had of the subjects under investigation.[41]

Neither of the objectives mentioned in the preceding paragraphs was achieved. As earlier discussion has shown, the committee went out of its way to mention individuals. Frequently its allusions and insinuations seemed intended solely to denigrate the character of persons for no other reason than that they disagreed with the committee's tactics. The objectives of the investigation were not furthered by reckless utterances that were patently false. As for the second objective, that of limiting the documents put into evidence to such "as seem absolutely necessary in order that a clear understanding might be had of the subjects under investigation," it is difficult to see how the contents of the four volumes referred to above meet this qualification.

There seems little point in devoting space to a discussion of most of the report because it bears so remotely upon the actual work of the committee. Some portions do call for comment, however, because they reflect the committee's penchant for labeling as subversive organizations which for one reason or another it did not approve. In a section entitled "revolutionary

[41] *Report of the Joint Legislative Committee of the State of New York Investigating Seditious Activities* (hereafter designated as *Report of Joint Legislative Committee*), I, 3.

industrial unionism" the committee included such organizations as the Industrial Workers of the World, the Brotherhood of Metal Workers' Industrial Union, the Amalgamated Clothing Workers of America, and the International Ladies' Garment Workers' Union.[42] To the committee, trade or craft unions were respectable, whereas industrial unions were subversive:

The movement thus created in the ranks of labor has been given many titles. In England it is known as syndicalism; in France as revolutionary syndicalism, while in the United States it has come to be known as industrial unionism. The object of the movement is to break up the system of craft or trade unions, and to organize workers into One Big Union having subdivisions along the lines of industry, rather than those of trade. The success of this movement is indicated in the following chapters of this sub-section.

The organizations thus created carry on their propaganda in co-operation with the propaganda of the so-called political organizations above referred to, the purpose of which is to create class consciousness, to stimulate in and among the workers the idea that they alone count in the social order; that only among the toiling masses is found the knowledge and ideals which can reconstruct society.

An intense hatred for all other classes of society is encouraged and the workers are urged to accentuate what is known as the class struggle. The purpose of this propaganda is to cultivate among workers, first, the desire and then the will to seize industry, and to overturn, or overthrow, organized government and to set up in its place the so-called cooperative commonwealth which now, in the minds of most of the workers affected by this propaganda, means a Soviet form of government modeled after the Russian Soviet regime.[43]

In the section dealing specifically with the Amalgamated Clothing Workers of America, the report states:

[42] *Report of Joint Legislative Committee,* I, 872–965.
[43] *Ibid.,* pp. 872–873.

Like all of the other subversive organizations its tactics are those of the class struggle. Its ultimate object is to take possession of the industry. Its principles and methods are almost identical with those of the Workingmen's International Industrial Union. It constitutes a typical example of revolutionary industrial unionism, being founded on the One Big Union idea.[44]

Equally suspect in the eyes of the committee were a number of pacifist organizations that functioned during the First World War. Its point of view is set forth in the Introduction to this section of the report:

It is the purpose of the Committee in the succeeding chapters of this section to show the use made by members of the Socialist Party of America and other extreme radicals and revolutionaries of pacifist sentiment among people of education and culture in the United States as a vehicle for the promotion of revolutionary Socialist propaganda. The facts here related are important because they show that these Socialists, playing upon the pacifist sentiment in a large body of sincere persons were able to organize their energies and to capitalize their prestige for the spread of their doctrines.

The group here treated is one of particular significance because it is recruited largely from among educators, authors, newspaper writers, and the clergy, thus giving entree to the public prints, influencing opinion, and invading public office during the war, also attempting to influence the foreign policy of this country toward Soviet Russia.[45]

Among the organizations whose activities were censured by the committee were the Emergency Peace Federation, the Ford Peace Party, the American Neutral Conference, the First American Conference for Democracy and Terms of Peace, the People's Council of the Americas, the American League to Limit Armaments, and the American Civil Liberties Union.[46]

[44] *Ibid.*, pp. 943–944.
[45] *Ibid.*, p. 969.
[46] *Ibid.*, pp. 971–1105.

In spite of the committee's "desire to eliminate personalities," it did not hesitate to single out for scathing criticism Louis P. Lochner, news correspondent, subsequently for many years chief of the Berlin Bureau of the Associated Press; Rosika Schwimmer, whose uncompromising advocacy of pacifism was later to be carried to the United States Supreme Court; and Jane Addams, a pioneer in American social work. Other well-known figures named by the committee included the lawyer and publicist Amos Pinchot, American Civil Liberties Union Director Roger Baldwin, David Starr Jordan, chancellor of Stanford University, Frederic C. Howe, author, teacher, and at that time Commissioner of Immigration of the Port of New York. The prominent Rabbi, Judah Magnes, leader of the Society for the Advancement of Judaism, was also included in Senator Lusk's list.

The American Civil Liberties Union seemed particularly offensive to the committee. Its records and those of its predecessor, the National Civil Liberties Bureau, were subpoenaed. From the bureau's voluminous files the committee reproduced thirty pages of documents and letters for its report.[47] Much of the data dealt with the work done on behalf of conscientious objectors during the First World War. The key to the committee's attitude is perhaps best expressed in its own observations:

It is worth noting further that the National Civil Liberties Bureau, under its new name of the American Civil Liberties Bureau [sic], today is as active as ever working up sympathy for revolutionaries, influencing public opinion, and generally spreading subversive propaganda.[48]

[47] *Ibid.*, pp. 1077–1104.

[48] *Ibid.*, p. 1095. For the informed student of public affairs, nothing could illustrate more graphically the fuzzy-minded character of the Lusk investigation than its indiscriminate labeling of the American Civil Liberties Union. Then as now that organization fought vigorously for the protection of civil liberties wherever and whenever they might come under attack. To confuse the

39

The activities of the Lusk committee have been reviewed briefly. There remains the task of testing the fruits of the investigation.

The Lusk Bills

The chairman recommended certain remedial legislation and introduced four bills to carry out his proposals. Two of the bills were protective in character: they were aimed at what the committee regarded as defective links in the chain of legal safeguards surrounding our educational system. The first bill provided that in addition to the existing qualifications, teachers must obtain a certificate of character. "Such certificates shall state that the teacher holding the same is a person of good moral character and that he has shown satisfactorily that he is obedient to and will support the constitutions and laws of this State and of the United States, and that he is desirous of the welfare of the country and in hearty accord and sympathy with the government and institutions of the State of New York and of the United States." The act also provided that the certificate could be revoked by the Commissioner of Education "on the ground that such person is not of good moral character, or for any act or utterance showing that he is not obedient to the constitutions and laws of this state or of the United States, or that he is not desirous of the welfare of the country or that he is not in hearty accord and sympathy with the government and institutions of this State or of the United States."

The second bill provided that no individual, group, or organization could establish or conduct a school or offer instruction without first receiving a license from the University of the State of New York, and no license was to be granted unless the Board of Regents were "satisfied that the instruction

issue by branding such activity as subversive was either unconscionably stupid or just plain vicious.

proposed to be given will not be detrimental to public interest." Such license "shall be revoked when it shall appear to the satisfaction of the regents that the school, institute, or class is being conducted in such manner as to be detrimental to public interests or is being conducted in a fraudulent or improper manner." This bill was patently directed against the Rand School.

The final two bills dealt with the problem of providing more comprehensive citizenship training for foreign-born and native adults. The first established teacher-training programs and the second directed the setting up in conjunction with factories and similar places of employment courses of instruction in English, history, civics, and other subjects promoting good citizenship. Both of these bills were admirable in aim, although it is apparent from the limited amount appropriated ($140,000 for both programs) that the problem of providing a workable state-wide training program had not been faced seriously.

The teachers' loyalty bill, though vigorously opposed by teachers' organizations and various citizens' groups, met an enthusiastic reception in the legislature. The Senate passed the measure with little comment, 43 to 8; the Assembly quickly added its approval with only three negative votes. A *New York Times* editorial apparently reflected public sentiment in general when it gave enthusiastic endorsement to the loyalty requirement.[49]

Reaction to the school license bill was more mixed. Many persons in and out of the legislature, while disagreeing sharply with the views and even the activities of the Rand School, gagged at this method of proscribing its work. Among other groups usually stamped as conservative, the New York City Bar Association added its protest to those of the Teachers Union and similar organizations which might naturally be

49 *New York Times,* April 22, 1920, p. 10.

expected to oppose the measure. Unlike the teachers' bill, the school license proposal did receive a thorough airing in both chambers. Although less one-sided, the vote was nevertheless more than enough for passage: 32 to 18 in the Senate and 100 to 30 in the Assembly.

Public interest in the Lusk bills reached its height in the period following legislative action. Members of the committee were active campaigners in support of the measures. They were effectively countered by numerous opposition groups. Governor Alfred E. Smith held a public hearing on the bills before reaching a decision. His veto message, a ringing denunciation of the thesis that the public safety can be guaranteed by repressive legislation, is a notable document in the literature of civil liberty. After declaring that the legislation was so defective that it could not possibly be enforced he continued:

I prefer, however, to rest my disapproval of it not solely nor chiefly on that ground, but on the broader ground that in fundamental principle the bill is vicious. Its avowed purpose is to safeguard the institutions and traditions of the country. In effect, it strikes at the very foundation of one of the most cardinal institutions of our nation—the fundamental right of the people to enjoy full liberty in the domain of idea and speech. To this fundamental right there is and can be under our system of government but one limitation, namely, that the law of the land shall not be transgressed, and there is abundant statute law prohibiting the abuse of free speech. It is unthinkable that in a representative democracy there should be delegated to any body of men the absolute power to prohibit the teaching of any subject of which it may disapprove.

The class of conflicting opinions, from which progress arises more than from any other source, would be abolished by law, tolerance and intellectual freedom destroyed, and an intellectual autocracy imposed upon the people. . . . The proponents of these bills urge that they are essential to the protection of the community against radical opinion. I might rest upon the saying of Benjamin Franklin that "they that can give up essential liberty to obtain a little temporary safety deserve neither liberty nor safety." But I go further—the safety of this government and its institutions rests upon the reasoned and devoted loyalty of its people. It does not need for its defense a system of intellectual tyranny which, in the endeavor to choke error by force, must of necessity crush truth as well. The profound sanity of the American people has been demonstrated in many a crisis, and I, for one, do not believe that governmental dictation of what may and may not be taught is necessary to achieve a continuance of the patriotism of our citizenship and its loyal support of the government and its institutions.[50]

Senator Lusk reintroduced his bills the following year (1920). They were approved in essentially the same form and readily signed by Governor Nathan L. Miller.[51] With the enactment of the school license bill, the fate of the Rand School again came to the fore. The school administration announced that it intended to ignore the Lusk Law and remain open without applying for a license. Attorney-General Newton was now in a position to achieve his earlier objective because he had a legal basis for closing the school. On July 15, 1922, his application for an injunction to prevent the school from operating without a license was granted on the ground that the statute requiring such license was valid.[52] Whether the Rand School was entitled to a license was not argued because the school steadfastly declined to make application.

Mr. Newton had not won his battle yet, however, for on October 7, 1922, the school was granted permission to remain

[50] *Public Papers of Governor Smith* (Albany, 1920), pp. 277 ff.
[51] *New York Times,* May 9, 1921, p. 5; *New York Laws,* 1921, c. 666, 667.
[52] *New York Times,* July 15, 1922, p. 1; *People v. American Socialist Society,* 202 App. Div. 640.

in operation pending final adjudication of the case by the Court of Appeals, New York's highest court.[53] With the re-election of Governor Smith the following month, on a Democratic platform pledged to repeal the Lusk laws, it became clear that further action in the courts would not be taken.

Shortly following the opening of the 1923 legislature, bills were introduced repealing the Lusk laws. Despite vigorous opposition by the Republican membership from upstate New York, which voted solidly against such action, the Lusk laws were repealed. The closeness of the contest is illustrated by the fact that on the first test the repealer was defeated in the Assembly because nine Democratic members were absent. On reconsideration, with all the Democrats present and voting for repeal, the Assembly approved the measure, 77 to 70.

Once more great clamor was raised as Governor Smith again called a public hearing. The most spectacular incident was the declaration by Dwight Braman, President of the Allied Patriotic Societies of New York, that within four months both the Congress and the state legislature would be convened in special session to take protective action against the Reds. Unimpressed by the arguments presented by Mr. Braman and his less fanciful associates, Governor Smith signed the repealer with the accompanying statement:

I am affixing my signature to the two acts which have for their purpose the repeal of the so-called Lusk laws. I am satisfied that they should not remain on the statute books of this state, because they are repugnant to the fundamentals of American democracy. Under the laws repealed, teachers in order to exercise their honorable calling, were in effect compelled to hold opinions as to governmental matters deemed by a State officer consistent with loyalty; and, further, no private school could be maintained in this state unless its teachings were similarly satisfactory to certain officials of the state. Freedom of opinion and freedom of speech

[53] *New York Times,* October 7, 1922, p. 3.

44

were by these laws unduly shackled, and unjust discrimination was made against the members of a great profession.

In signing these bills, I firmly believe that I am vindicating the principle that, within the limits of the Penal Law, every citizen may speak and teach what he believes.[54]

Public Reaction: Apathy or Fear?

The extreme measures taken by the Lusk committee and the Assembly are in themselves shocking, but the point which particularly disturbs is the almost complete absence of protest, except from the American Civil Liberties Union and a few left-wing labor groups. The tendency of the legislative committee to permit its zeal to blur its sense of proportion can be understood. It has happened before and is likely to happen again. But the committee could not have abused its responsibility so flagrantly had it not received wholehearted co-operation from the executive and judicial branches of the government—co-operation which cannot be regarded as anything less than collusion because it involved either the evasion or the distortion of legal and constitutional provisions. Yet the citizenry witnessed this subversion of the law with almost no protest. What accounts for this supine behavior? Was it apathy or fear, or did public silence reflect general approbation of what was taking place?

Answers to this question are not readily at hand because the public as a whole does not find easy means for making its view articulate. Certain facts must be kept in mind, however. The Lusk investigation cannot be separated from the setting in which it occurred: a postwar period with all its maladjustments; turmoil at home in the form of major labor unrest; complete disharmony between the President and Congress concerning the peace treaties and America's position in the Western world; Russia in chaos and its convulsions inducing

[54] *Ibid.*, May 26, 1923, p. 17.

secondary shock in both the international and domestic aspects of American recuperation. Most Americans were concentrating upon their own personal problems—trying to regain momentum after having been stalled or sidetracked for a couple of years. Their chief concern was personal, not political, certainly not international. On the other hand, those who were troubled by what was going on in the world—at home and abroad—were those who could always see two witches in every bush for one that was actually there. Whether their motives were wholly honorable is impossible to say because it seems doubtful if they themselves could tell, but it is probably a matter of only minor importance anyway. The point worthy of emphasis is that with the extremists at the throttle and the general public silent, there was no counterweight to check the momentum of the vehicle as it careened so recklessly off course.

In times of social unrest when self-appointed and self-assured champions of the public safety accuse particular individuals or groups of subverting cherished institutions, the position of the innocent bystander is both difficult and embarrassing. Usually he stands by, silent and uncomfortable, an unhappy but seemingly acquiescent witness to actions which he disapproves.

It is easy to use the term "apathy" in such instances, but perhaps that labeling is just a shade too pat. Is it apathy when one refrains from crying out at some unfair accusation because of fear that protest will call down upon his own head retaliatory action from the agency whose action he deplores? Thoughtful observers of the unrestrained activities of legislative fishing expeditions have shrewdly pointed out that an almost inevitable by-product of the free-swinging legislative investigation—whether deliberately so designed or not—is its intimidating effect upon the general public.

When to protest smear tactics is to invite such procedures against oneself or family, the less valorous course of remaining

46

silent hardly deserves the harsh epithet "apathy." The melancholy fact remains: it is only from the legislative branch that we have been unable to protect ourselves against such abuses of governmental power that the private citizen fears to speak out against arbitrary action.

For those who frighten easily, there were ample signs of danger. From coast to coast there was labor strife. The IWW's, a militant organization not averse at that time to employing violence in furthering its cause, was at the peak of its striking power. Just as the committee began its activity, a series of nationwide bombings occurred and a wave of hysteria swept across the country. Within a short time Attorney-General Palmer embarked upon his wholesale Red hunt aimed at the forced deportation of hundreds of allegedly dangerous aliens. These events, liberally seasoned by daily dispatches from Russia describing scenes of barbarity, established an atmosphere in which emotional factors far outweighed sober judgment.

It is interesting to note that the excesses of the Lusk committee received general newspaper support. Editorial comment in the *New York Times* gave the investigation as prosecuted full backing. The following extract from a *Times* editorial is typical:

Of all the many efforts which the Rand School has been making to extend its seditious propaganda, none will or should incite more vehement indignation than that to undermine the loyalty of the Negroes. Documents laid before the Lusk Committee prove conclusively, not that the efforts were successful, indeed, but that they were elaborate and determined as well as utterly ruthless, and that they involved the expenditure of money in considerable amounts. The leader of this branch of the school's work is himself a Negro but presumably is not an American Negro, as his name is Domingo, and by the cynical contempt he expressed for the character and intelligence of Negro preachers, he showed how far

47

he is from respecting the standards accepted by most American Negroes. He described them as "owned body and soul by the capitalist class." [55]

The Unseating of the Five Socialist Assemblymen

Before the Lusk committee completed its work, the controversy over the seating of five Socialist members of the Assembly absorbed both the attention of the general public and the energies of the investigating committee staff.

Early in 1920, while Senator Lusk and his associates were still engaged in conducting sporadic raids upon the headquarters of "dangerous" radical organizations, the New York Assembly suddenly attracted nationwide attention by voting 140 to 6 to deny five persons duly elected to the Assembly the privilege of taking their seats "pending determination of their qualifications and eligibility." As members of the Socialist Party of America "which supported the principles of Soviet Communism" these assemblymen, so it was argued, were not qualified to hold office.

The action taken against the five assemblymen as well as the procedure by which it was taken was unprecedented. When the New York Assembly convened on January 7, 1920, the five Socialist members-elect, four of whom had previously served in the Assembly, presented themselves, took the oath of office, and occupied their seats, without protest or question. As duly sworn members, they participated in organizing the Assembly and voted in the election of the Speaker and other officers.

After proceedings had been under way for approximately two hours, the newly elected Speaker, without warning or explanation, suddenly directed the sergeant-at-arms to present the five Socialist members before the bar. The five men were herded before the Speaker's rostrum like pickpockets before

[55] *Ibid.,* June 30, 1919, p. 10.

a police magistrate and were informed that they had been elected on a platform inimical to the best interests of the state and nation. No specific charges were lodged against the alleged offenders, other than the fact of their membership in the Socialist Party (a legally recognized party under the state election law), but a resolution denying them their seats was presented to the Assembly. Under the terms of the resolution the accused assemblymen were to be unseated until the Judiciary Committee should investigate and report upon their eligibility. The resolution was drafted by Attorney-General Newton. During the trial that ensued, Mr. Newton was assisted by Samuel A. Berger and Archibald E. Stevenson, two of the most active members of the Lusk committee staff.

The action of the New York Assembly was arbitrary and illegal, in spite of the fact that the Speaker of the Assembly, who engineered the coup, and the Judiciary Committee, which conducted the hearings, went to great pains to establish the fiction of regularity by elaborate procedural apparatus.[56]

In the course of examining the charges against the Socialist

---

[56] The trial of the five Socialist assemblymen—for that is what the proceedings amounted to—was undoubtedly colored by the action taken against Congressman-elect Victor Berger by the United States House of Representatives. It is perhaps only a coincidence, but every New York legislative investigation of un-American practices has followed closely upon the heels of a similar congressional excursion into the same field. The precedent of the Berger case cannot be ignored, although the facts in the two cases were quite different. While under indictment for conspiracy under the Espionage Act, Victor Berger was elected to Congress from Wisconsin on the Socialist ticket. Subsequent to his election Berger was tried, convicted, and sentenced to twenty years' imprisonment. Pending appeal, he was released on bail, and when the new Congress convened he presented himself but was denied his seat. After some months' investigation by a special committee, the House declared Berger's seat vacant in November, 1919. Within a month, at a special election, Berger was re-elected by a considerably increased margin only to have the House of Representatives once more refuse to seat him on January 10, 1920.

The New York Assembly instituted its action against its five Socialist members just ten days after the House of Representatives had for the second time voted to exclude Mr. Berger.

assemblymen, the Judiciary Committee conducted proceedings with great punctilio. For six weeks the Committee sat in judgment while counsel for both sides presented elaborate formal argument. The highly legalistic quality of most of the argument on either side was in striking contrast to the strictly extralegal character of the proceeding itself.

After amassing a record of more than twenty-eight hundred pages with an additional five hundred pages of exhibits and documents, the Judiciary Committee submitted its report. By a vote of seven to six, the Committee recommended that the seats of the five suspended assemblymen be declared vacant. In the two months since the initial action by the Assembly some of its members had reconsidered their positions, but the shift was not significant. The Socialists were denied their seats by votes ranging from 115 to 78 to 104 to 40, each case being voted upon separately.

There was no authority in the constitution or statutes of the state for suspending the Socialists, pending determination of their eligibility to retain their seats. Equally lacking was any authority for expelling them when no charges of personal misconduct (overt acts as distinguished from opinions or affiliations) had been lodged against them.

In New York the power of the legislature to expel a member is conferred by statute, but neither the constitution nor the statutes provide for suspension of a member. There are many precedents, both state and national, that after an elected legislator has once taken the oath of office he is entitled to retain his seat and exercise all rights and privileges. Even if charges are preferred against him and he is investigated, tried, and eventually expelled, he continues to exercise his rights until the vote expelling him has actually been taken.

The action of the Assembly offended not only because it was taken without authority; it actually violated the state constitution in at least two respects. The constitution requires of all state officers a customary oath of office pledging support of the Constitution of the United States and that of the State of New York. But the constitution also provides, "No other oath, declaration or test shall be required as a qualification for any office of public trust." At another place the constitution provides that no member of the state shall be disfranchised unless by the law of the land or the judgment of his peers. Both of these prohibitions were violated by the actions taken against the Socialists. While the constitution makes each house of the legislature the judge of the qualifications of its members, the provisions just mentioned place well-defined limitations upon the scope of this authority. Clearly, the Assembly had no authority to establish additional qualifications and then expel duly elected persons for failure to meet the new requirements. Yet this is precisely what it did. Similarly, through its illegal suspension and subsequent expulsion of the five Socialist assemblymen, the Assembly actually disfranchised sixty thousand voters in New York City because they were unrepresented in the lower chamber during the entire legislative session.

The ease with which the Assembly could disregard so completely the basic principles which alone give meaning to our political institutions is the most disturbing aspect of this episode. One must conclude that the spirit which was reflected in the operations of the Lusk committee cannot be discounted as that of an insignificant, irresponsible minority. The political temper of the legislature as a whole seemed to harmonize well with the actions of its agents.[57]

Concluding Observations upon the Lusk Committee

It is doubtful if there ever was another investigation like that carried on by the Lusk committee. From the beginning it

[57] For a fuller account of the exclusion of the five New York Socialists, see Z. Chafee, *Free Speech in the United States* (Cambridge, Mass., 1941), pp. 269–282.

functioned more like a combination police force and district attorney's office than a legislative investigating committee. Undoubtedly part of the explanation for the odd behavior of the committee can be traced to its organization. When Senator Lusk chose as chief counsel for his committee the Attorney-General of the state, the character of the investigation was fundamentally influenced. At the outset the inquiry was placed in an anomalous and contradictory position, because of the confusion of legislative and executive personnel, hence of viewpoints, objectives, and methods. Before the investigation was completed, the third division of government—the judiciary—entered the scene to confuse matters further. In its day-to-day operations the committee was never clear whether it was a fact-finding body, a prosecuting agency, or a police force. Indeed, at times it seemed to regard itself more as a propaganda bureau than anything else. The decision to operate through the Attorney-General's office was unfortunate. It deprived the committee of that spirit of detachment so important if a fact-finding job is to be discharged faithfully. Instead, the point of view of the Attorney-General's office prevailed, and the committee abandoned the investigative function before it ever got started.

II

Loyalty Laws and Investigations

1934-1939

B ETWEEN the events of the Lusk era and the second full-
scale investigation twenty years later, the most significant
New York State legislative action in the field of un-American
activities is represented by the Ives Loyalty Oath Law, the
abortive McNaboe investigations, and the Devany Law. Each
of these will be discussed briefly.

The Ives Loyalty Oath Law

In 1934 Assembly Majority Leader (now United States
Senator) Irving M. Ives introduced a bill requiring all teachers
to take a loyalty oath. Actually, all newly appointed public
school teachers in New York City had been required to take
such an oath for many years. The oath, which dated back to
the First World War, had crept into the regulations of the
New York City Board of Education, although no statutory
authority could be found for such a rule. The Ives bill did not
explicitly identify the categories of teachers to which it applied, and Governor Lehman emphasized this ambiguity as
one of the defects which prompted him to veto the bill.

Later in the same year an extraordinary session of the legislature provided Mr. Ives with another opportunity to put his bill over. An amended bill required teachers in all public schools and in private schools operating on tax-exempt property to subscribe to the following oath: "I do solemnly swear (or affirm) that I will support the Constitution of the United States and the Constitution of the State of New York, and that I will faithfully discharge, to the best of my ability, the duties of the position to which I am now assigned."

Although the bill was vigorously attacked by teacher groups and the American Civil Liberties Union on the grounds that teachers should not be singled out for special treatment, the Assembly approved it, 129 to 8, and the Senate, 40 to 2. Governor Lehman signed the bill, explaining that some of his original objections had been met and saying that there was "very strong sentiment in its favor among the teachers themselves." The statute remains in force today.

The Ives Loyalty Oath Law, hailed by its author and its supporters as the best antidote to "too much teaching of various 'isms' in the schools," did not obviate the necessity of two legislative investigations of subversive activities in the schools within the next half dozen years. Sporadic bills attacking or seeking to investigate alleged subversive movements have been a characteristic feature of each legislative session.

Beginning in 1936, however, the tempo and intensity of this form of legislative activity showed a marked increase. Early in the 1936 session bills were introduced which would (1) require a loyalty oath to the state and federal governments from all students before they could be admitted to any high school or college supported in whole or in part by public funds (this bill had been approved by the Senate in 1935 only to die in the Assembly); (2) bar state aid to any educational institution where "destructive doctrines such as communism, Bolshevism and other radical theories are taught and encouraged"; (3) require the display of the American flag in all public school classrooms; and (4) require school busses to be painted red, white, and blue.

The flag display bill was overwhelmingly approved by the Senate. The vote of 48 to 2 seemed to reflect the sentiment expressed by Senator (later Lieutenant Governor) Joe R. Hanley when he observed, "We want people to respect the flag and if they will not respect it voluntarily, then we will make them respect it involuntarily." In the Assembly either a different conception of fostering patriotism prevailed or less faith was vested in the potence of legislative fiat, for the bill was killed by an almost unanimous vote. The bill was later modified to require only that the flag be displayed in the assembly hall of every public school. In this form it passed and became law when approved by the governor.

Hearings were held on the student loyalty oath bill with a large number of organizations pressing arguments on either side. The proposal did not come up for a vote in either chamber.

The McNaboe Investigations

The most significant legislative expression of concern for un-American activities during this period was presented by the McNaboe resolution. Introduced early in the regular session of 1936 by Senator John J. McNaboe of New York City, the resolution, which called for an appropriation of $150,000, reviewed a broad range of un-American activities allegedly being carried on by students and faculty in New York schools. In the closing moments of the special session Senator McNaboe succeeded in pushing his bill through both houses but only with a much reduced appropriation. The resolution carrying an appropriation of $15,000 was approved in the Senate 26 to 10 and in the Assembly 119 to 21. The resolution received Governor Herbert Lehman's approval on July 9, 1936.

The language of the long resolution is revealing and casts doubt upon the objective quality of the inquiry. The enumeration of alleged abuses or undesirable conditions states categorically that they exist, thus converting the proposed investigation into a prosecution before it had been authorized.[1]

From the middle of July when the committee was created until the end of the following January when it had been directed to report, it never held a single session. Initial difficulty occurred when some legislators appointed to the committee refused to serve because they believed its methods would violate individual liberty. Further complications appeared when Republican members of the committee begged off because of the exigencies of the political campaign then under way. Although the first public hearing was officially announced for October 29, 1936, neither the chairman nor the committee counsel appeared, and another meeting was never scheduled. During the fall and winter Senator McNaboe made several public statements which did much to cast suspicion upon the whole venture. At one time and another he charged that various educational institutions, including Cornell University, New York University, Teachers College of Columbia University, and various of the colleges and public schools of New York City were "hot beds of communism." In one characteristic outburst, he asserted that Cornell was a

[1] Representative excerpts from the resolution are included for illustrative purposes. For the entire resolution see Appendix II.

"Whereas, Our students are daily exposed to seditious or treasonable utterances in literature openly circulated in school rooms, assembly halls, on the campus and in school official publications, as well as from the lips of faculty members, and

"Whereas, Professional paid agitators and propagandists are intimidating students in order to force their alliance with a so-called 'United Front' that purposes to overthrow our Constitutional form of government and establish 'a new social order,' said end to be gained through revolutionary tactics, admittedly illegal and unconstitutional," etc., etc.

"center of revolutionary communistic propaganda" and added that he had "documentary evidence beyond any question whatever." On a later occasion he declared that the Communists were plotting to massacre the New York City police.

As time went on, the Senator broadened his accusations. He charged that the American Civil Liberties Union was closely affiliated with the Communist movement and that it devoted fully 90 per cent of its efforts in behalf of Communists who had come into conflict with the law. Simultaneously, Mr. McNaboe made veiled and contradictory allusions to the reasons for his committee's failure to function. A hint that party patronage demands had eaten up the committee appropriation was followed by the statement that because of behind-the-scene politics the committee had not been able to spend a penny. At any rate, by the time its date of expiration had arrived, this particular investigation had produced nothing except a welter of unsubstantiated charges of a thoroughly sensational and irresponsible character. For this abortive episode the chairman alone was accountable because the committee had never had so much as an organization meeting.

It is little wonder that the legislature permitted the investigation to die, but this did not occur until Senator McNaboe had his final inning. In an effort to have the committee revived and extended, he obtained the floor on a point of high personal privilege and reiterated previously made charges that his investigation was being killed by Mayor La Guardia because of fear of disclosures of communism running rife in the New York City schools. He later linked La Guardia with the Russian-American Industrial Corporation, which he said was instrumental in industrializing the Soviet Union. When questioned further why his committee had thus far failed to function, he replied, "The reason I am not answering that question is because I am a regular Democrat, right down the line. No one in the future will be able to challenge my party allegiance.

57

That is the answer." Senator Jacob Livingston, vice-chairman of the committee, also a Democrat, termed McNaboe's charges against La Guardia ridiculous and added that because of his statements the committee had become the laughing stock of the country and should be allowed to die.

Through a strange combination of circumstances, Senator McNaboe managed to achieve his objective by indirection. In May, 1937, shortly following the demise of his un-American activities investigation, he succeeded in pushing through the legislature a resolution establishing a joint committee to investigate the administration and enforcement of the law with special emphasis upon the treatment of persons on parole. The resolution carried an appropriation of $20,000. When Governor Lehman vetoed the appropriation, it appeared that the investigating Senator had been balked again, but not for long. During the summer of 1937 a series of murders involving children occurred. After the murder of a four-year-old girl in a particularly brutal sex crime, Senator McNaboe called upon Senator Dunnigan, Temporary President of the Senate, and Speaker of the Assembly Heck to release funds from the legislative contingent fund in order that his investigation might proceed. Under considerable pressure because of the temporarily aroused public opinion, the legislative leaders announced that they were authorizing the requested allocation of funds.

The specific language of the resolution in question carried no hint that it was to be concerned with anything other than criminal law enforcement and the treatment of such related matters as probation, parole, and mental hygiene. One paragraph was broad enough to cover almost any area of activity, however:

The investigation of such committee may include every matter and thing not specifically mentioned in this resolution deemed by

58

the committee competent, relevant and material in the ascertainment of the true situation respecting the intent and purpose of these resolutions or intended so to be, as though specific provision and authority therefore had been expressly granted herein.

The McNaboe committee held fifteen public hearings between the end of September, 1937, and the opening of the next session of the legislature in 1938. These hearings were devoted exclusively to problems clearly within the purview of the resolution and the committee was continued with an additional appropriation of $40,000. Eight more sessions in 1938 dealt with criminal law enforcement, but beginning in the middle of May, the committee abruptly shifted its focus. From that date forward the committee concentrated its attack upon various aspects of what it termed un-American activities. No pretense was made of prosecuting a systematic inquiry. For the next month and a half a variety of witnesses were interrogated on one or another phase of communism and fascism.

It is difficult to speak with certainty concerning the motives and causes which produced the new tack in the committee's course. As in the case of its resuscitation the preceding year, a combination of events and circumstances which actually bore only remotely upon the committee's assignment provided an excuse for its excursion into threats to the American form of government.

Early in 1938, newly elected Borough of Manhattan President Stanley Isaacs appointed as one of his aides Simon Gerson, a member of the Communist Party and a reporter on the *Daily Worker*. The appointment had occasioned widespread comment, much of it critical. Various groups, including the New York State American Legion, continued an unrestrained campaign of censure after the general public had ceased to give the incident much attention. In the middle of March Senator McNaboe was the coauthor of identical bills introduced in both houses barring from civil service and teaching positions any person who espoused the overthrow of the government by force, etc. In introducing his bill, Senator McNaboe took occasion to criticize Mr. Isaacs for the appointment of Gerson.

Notwithstanding widespread editorial attack and concerted opposition from various civic and business groups, the McNaboe bill received affirmative votes of 39 to 3 in the Senate and 110 to 22 in the Assembly, only to be killed by Governor Lehman in a strongly worded veto on March 30, 1938. Senator McNaboe was bitter over his defeat; he charged publicly that Supreme Court Justice Charles Poletti, whom he called "Communistic Charlie" and the tool of Roger Baldwin, was responsible for the veto and had in fact written the veto message.

When an enterprising reporter turned up the information that in a civil proceeding in the Municipal Court involving Simon Gerson, his name had been reported as Samuel Gilson, McNaboe was provided an opening. The action was a civil one involving a technical point in connection with the Multiple Dwelling Law. Absolutely no question of party activity or even of Gerson's conduct in his borough office post was involved, but it was enough for Senator McNaboe.

A hearing was called to interrogate the judge and attorney concerned and from that opening gambit the inquiry broadened out to include a grilling of Gerson on his Communist views and of Isaacs upon his motives for appointing a Communist to public office. Subsequently, the committee interrogated assorted members of the German-American Bund and Communist Earl Browder. An examination of the 329 pages of testimony devoted to this phase of the inquiry comes close to revealing the worst faults of the investigative function: aimless, irrelevant, unrelated questions betraying extreme personal prejudice; vague interrogatories defying satisfactory answers; badgering of witnesses; misinterpretation of witnesses' answers, whether deliberate or because of no comprehension on the part of the interrogator.

Failure of the committee to select a counsel equipped to plan, prepare, and conduct a systematic inquiry was at least an important contributory factor in its inept performance. The hearings elicited nothing because the committee did not seem to know what it was looking for and certainly did not know how to go about getting it. The McNaboe committee terminated its work by recommending that legislation be enacted to "outlaw the Communist Party" and to bar from public office all members of the Communist Party. Nothing in the genesis, procedure, or product of the McNaboe committee distinguishes it as a constructive undertaking.

In conclusion, a word about the documentary record of the investigation may be useful. Two volumes of hearings and exhibits, totaling 2,355 pages, constitute the final report. Of this total, 973 pages are devoted to the enforcement of the criminal law, the subject for which the committee was created.[2] The remaining 1,382 pages present a hodgepodge of miscellaneous material on subversive activities, a subject not within the committee's jurisdiction.

The materials in the second volume of the report of the Joint Legislative Committee to Investigate the Administration and Enforcement of the Law (Legislative Document [1939], No. 98, Exhibits) are comprised chiefly of copies of the *Daily Worker* and such institutional publications as the *X-Ray* (Bellevue), *New York Hospital Worker* (New York Hospital), *Educational Vanguard* (Teachers College), *Teacher and Worker* (City College), *The Staff* (Brooklyn College), *The Challenge* (Evander Childs High School), *Student Front* (Cornell University), and treatises or pamphlets on communism by Browder, Bittleman, M. J. Ogin, and others. All of this ma-

2 *New York Legislative Documents,* 162nd Session, 1939, Vol. XXIII, No. 98.

terial was readily available without reproduction. None of it was secret or difficult to get.

To conclude that the McNaboe investigations produced harmful results would be to credit them with more definite achievement than the facts seem to warrant. Only on the assumption that a dissipation of public funds without producing any constructive report is harmful would one be justified in such a judgment. Actually the investigations never carried enough impact to do real damage. If they had been pushed with vigor and resourcefulness, the situation might have been different, because the chairman did not exhibit that sense of responsibility and self-restraint which any legislative investigation demands if it is to realize its objectives. The other members of the committee, while decidedly less extreme, showed little more conception of their objective and no more skill in achieving it.

One cannot review such abuse of governmental power by officials acting under color of its authority without experiencing a deep sense of shame. But what is the cost in terms of respect for our institutions and the democratic process through which these institutions find expression? Is the injury suffered at the hands of an arrogant or ignorant legislative investigator measurable only in terms of personal pain and spiritual depression, or does the incident exact more pervasive toll in its impact upon our institutions and our civic values?

How many McNaboe investigations does it take to blur the public's general sense of justice? How much invective, abuse, and extravagant allegation can an official emit before the general public finds its attention dulled and repelled? The time comes when cynicism replaces discrimination and serious reflection gives way to indifference—a state in which democratic institutions cannot function. Here, it is submitted, lies the danger in even such fiascoes as the McNaboe investigation. The burlesque character of much of the proceedings quickly became apparent to those who took the trouble to keep up with its splashy headlines. Yet officially the McNaboe investigation was a bona fide legislative enterprise. In what way can it be said that respect either for human dignity or the integrity of the democratic process was strengthened by this episode?

The Devany Law

Senator McNaboe's persistence finally paid dividends, although perhaps not in such handsome fashion as he had hoped. What he was not able to achieve directly came about at least partly as a reflex to his own efforts. The Devany Law barring from public office or public educational institutions persons supporting the overthrow of government by violence might not have been approved had it not been for the much more extreme McNaboe bill. The circumstances surrounding the enactment of this legislation grew directly out of Senator McNaboe's own abortive effort.

Early in the 1939 session of the legislature, Senator McNaboe introduced the legislation which Governor Lehman had vetoed the preceding year. His bill, popularly termed the "anti-Red" bill, barred Communists from any civil service position. It defined "Communist" in such broad terms that many persons who in no sense advocated the violent overthrow of government would fall within its language. The New York League of Women Voters and the Citizens' Union of New York City immediately attacked the bill on the grounds that it was attempting to employ totalitarian methods to defend democratic institutions and that its ultimate effect would be to suppress civil liberties and academic freedom rather than to protect them. Others based their criticism upon the fact that while the bill proscribed public employment of Communists, nothing was said about Fascists or Nazis. This group, which included the New York State American Legion and other powerful organizations, indicated that they were not opposed to

63

all such legislation. The inference was left that their objections could be met by more careful drafting. The Devany bill which had been introduced in the Assembly seemed to be the answer.

This bill was similar in that it also contemplated the exclusion from public office of persons advocating or teaching that the government "should be overthrown by force, violence, or any unlawful means." It also applied specifically to Communists, but its language was broad enough to cover all foreign "isms." The American Legion officially endorsed this measure. Several state senators who opposed the McNaboe bill found the Devany bill less objectionable; they indicated that they might support Senator McNaboe's proposal should he modify it along these lines.

The Senator was adamant. He insisted that the real threat to democracy was communism and he did not wish to be deflected from his objective by having his bill broadened to include other dangerous groups. He explained that a subsequent bill would deal with Nazis and Fascists but that the present measure should stand as drafted. Apparently the Senator knew his colleagues because his bill was approved 27 to 20 on March 13, 1939.

The party voting on the bill is interesting. All Republicans present voted for the bill and were joined by four Democrats. Three Republicans were absent when the vote was taken. Of these, one, Senator Desmond, had previously expressed strong opposition, not only to the McNaboe bill specifically but to all legislation of this kind. Senator Coudert, later to head the investigation of the New York City schools, was among those voting favorably. Senator Joe R. Hanley, Republican majority leader, made special point of emphasizing, however, that the McNaboe bill was not a party measure.[3]

Senator Hanley's statement was given added point a week

3 *New York Times*, March 14, 1939, pp. 1, 10.

later when Speaker Oswald D. Heck expressed his strong opposition to both the McNaboe and Devany bills and declared that he did not want the Republican Party to support any legislation of this character. The fate of the McNaboe bill was sealed when it was buried in the Assembly Rules Committee, but other Republican assemblymen indicated that they did not share Mr. Heck's views concerning the Devany bill. If certain amendments were made, clarifying its language and strengthening the procedural safeguards to prevent abuse, they predicted party support.

Mr. Devany incorporated the proposed changes in his bill. The pertinent provisions (Section 12-a of the New York civil service law) follow:

No person shall be employed in the service of the state nor as a superintendent, principal, or teacher in a public school or state normal school or college or any other state educational institution who a) By word of mouth or writing wilfully and deliberately advocates, advises or teaches the doctrine that the government of the United States or any state or of any subdivision thereof should be overthrown or overturned by force, violence or any unlawful means.

Subdivision b forbids the publication of articles for the above purpose. Subdivision c forbids the organization or joining of any group for the above purpose. Subdivision d establishes certain procedural safeguards:

A person dismissed or declared ineligible may within four months of such dismissal or declaration of ineligibility be entitled to petition for an order to show cause signed by a justice of the Supreme Court, why a hearing on such charge should not be had. Until the final judgment on such hearing is entered, the order to show cause shall stay the effect of any order of dismissal or ineligibility based on the provisions of this section. The hearing shall consist of the taking of testimony in open court with opportunity for cross examination. The burden of sustaining the validity of the order of dismissal or ineligibility by a fair preponderance of the credible evidence shall be upon the person making such dismissal or order of ineligibility.

In this form the bill was given strong support in the Assembly. On final passage the vote of 107 to 27 did not follow party lines. Although most Republicans supported the bill, they were joined by many Democrats; on the other hand, some of the most prominent Republican leaders of the Assembly, among them Speaker Heck, Majority Leader Ives, and Abbot Low Moffat, voted against passage.[4] Three weeks later the Senate approved the Devany bill 39 to 6, Senator Desmond being the lone Republican to oppose.

Completion of legislative action on the Devany bill gave rise to wide speculation over Governor Lehman's position. His vigorous veto message of the previous year was still fresh in public memory. On the other hand, it was recalled that five years earlier he had vetoed the first Ives bill and then had approved a similar measure on the ground that through more careful drafting some of its more objectionable features had been removed. If he so wished, the Governor could again take this way out because no one could deny that the Devany bill was superior to its predecessor.

The Governor's long statement approving the measure suggested a somewhat labored attempt on his part to justify his retreat from his earlier, more forthright position. He stressed the procedural safeguards present in the new bill and pointed out that the United States Supreme Court had already upheld sections of the New York Penal Law that prohibited acts such as those included in this bill. His insistence that he had not changed his position would have been more persuasive had not the language of his earlier veto been so uncompromising.

[4] *Ibid.*, April 20, 1939, pp. 1, 2.

The Devany Law was, to be sure, a vast improvement over the McNaboe bill which it replaced. Still it fell short of meeting the standards of the democracy it purportedly sought to protect. It intruded into the field of public employment an issue of political belief which was unrelated to efficiency and to the faithfulness with which particular duties might be discharged. It undertook to penalize mere advocacy, unconnected with activity of a lawless character. It forbade teaching or writing about doctrines which the legislature thought detestable. Statutory command replaced professional judgment concerning the suitability of teachers in colleges and schools. Thus, as enacted, the measure embodied concepts which are rejected by those who believe in the power of democratic institutions and who cherish civil liberties and academic freedom as elements of that power. Unlike the McNaboe bill, however, the Devany Law embodied carefully detailed procedural safeguards. It offends substantively but in so doing preserves meticulously the procedural amenities.[5]

[5] *New York Laws,* 1939, c. 547. Actually, the Devany Law was not invoked in the removal of teachers following the Rapp-Coudert investigation of 1940–1941. (See p. 169.) In 1949, however, the Feinberg Law amplified and sharpened the procedural provisions of the Devany Law. (See pp. 191–193.)

III

The Rapp-Coudert Investigation

THE fortuitous origin of the McNaboe investigation has already been related. Oddly enough the legislative investigation of subversive activities in the New York City schools, during 1940–1941, popularly known as the Rapp-Coudert investigation, had somewhat the same genesis, although under conditions less objectionable, as will be indicated later.

Conditions in the city schools had been the source of complaint for many reasons and from many quarters. In a sense, all difficulties could be traced to financial causes, although in some instances the financial factor was immediate and direct, while in others it was more remote and contributory. Inadequate funds had led to unwise personnel policies in all of the tax-supported schools. In the elementary and high schools recourse had been taken to the systematic employment of substitute teachers in order to spread the salary dollar over more teaching capacity. Evasion of salary increases and withholding of deserved tenure produced low morale and insecurity among the instructional staff.

Administrative officials in the city colleges followed different methods, but the result was the same. By creating new titles such as reader and tutor, they were able to take advantage of a depressed economic situation to hire college teachers for a third or a half of the officially recognized salary rate. Numerous instances could be cited of individuals with outstanding records of scholarship who had completed their professional training and several years of successful college teaching, yet were receiving less than $1,500 a year.

Faced with the problem of bettering their economic position, the instructional officers below the rank of assistant professor formed the Instructional Staff Association for the purpose of presenting an organized case. Similar, although more complex, motives lay behind the activity of Local 5, AFL, the Teachers Union, and, later, of Local 537, AFL, the College Teachers Union. There can be no doubt that in the case of each of these organizations the underlying motive of the organization itself and of the vast majority of those who joined it was that of improving the economic and professional position of teachers.

Financial pressure thus lay at the base of much of the alleged subversive activity which the Rapp-Coudert committee was directed to investigate, although the scope of inquiry of the subcommittee on subversive activities in New York City schools did not extend into financial matters, even to a small degree. Originally, however, and again ultimately, as later evidence will indicate, the legislative intent in creating an investigative committee had been exclusively financial.

New York City schools have long been financed jointly by the city and the state. Roughly 70 per cent of the school budget has come from local taxes, with the remaining 30 per cent coming from the state on the basis of formulae which have been modified from time to time but which have usually been based primarily upon student attendance.

The combination of falling assessed valuation of real property and increasing unit educational costs because of reduced enrollment in New York City schools precipitated a two-way squeeze on school revenues which outran the slight reduction in educational expenditures occasioned by falling enrollment.

Existing formulae for determining the amount and equitable allocation of state aid to education were obsolete. Legislators from all parts of the state were largely in agreement with professional school people that the whole subject of state financial aid to education needed thorough study before new legislation should be attempted.

To this end a resolution by Senator Herbert A. Rapp in March, 1940, concerned solely with the problem of school finances, had been approved by both the Senate and the Assembly before the issue of subversive activities had been introduced.[1]

To this original resolution, retained in its entirety, a single new subsection was added. The addition soon became a case of the tail wagging the dog, because for the next two years the initial and larger problem of educational finance was sidetracked by the subversive activity investigation. Not until 1942 did the committee get back to the study for which it had been created. But before the work of the subversive activities committee is examined, it is appropriate to sketch briefly the events preceding its establishment.

Partly because of financial difficulties already alluded to and partly because of questionable personnel practices, the presidents of both City College and Hunter College had encountered considerable friction in the administration of their respective institutions. In each instance, for a variety of reasons, significant sections of the faculty and of the Board of Higher Education were out of sympathy with the existing arrangement. By a series of incidents which it seems unnecessary to review here, both President Robinson of City College and President Colligan of Hunter College ceased to continue in office.

These events occurred in 1938 and 1939. In both instances some segments of the general public supported the ousted of-

---

[1] For the text of the Rapp resolution, see Appendix V.

ficials, and the Board's handling of the matter was subjected to bitter criticism. The issue of communism was not greatly stressed at this time, although the outspoken opposition to President Robinson by the Teachers Union, which was regarded in some quarters as a Communist organization, produced the charge that his removal had been influenced by the Communist Party. Similarly, one of the rumors accompanying President Colligan's departure was that his views were too conservative to please certain of the liberals on the board.

Action in the Legislature

The entire question of conditions in the schools was suddenly brought into the limelight at this time by the appointment of Bertrand Russell as professor of philosophy in City College. The eminent British philosopher and mathematician was a controversial figure. His unorthodox views on the conventional canons of morality, particularly the institution of marriage, had been severely criticized by high officials of the Roman Catholic Church. Few issues have caused a greater clamor. Sentiment was by no means unanimous, but the opposition, much more vocal and intense, made the stronger showing. The legislature then in session gave the subject full play and lost no time in aligning itself with the opposition. On March 22, 1940, the Senate passed the Phelps resolution protesting Russell's appointment. A few minutes later Senator John H. Dunnigan of New York City introduced a resolution calling for a sweeping investigation of the entire New York City school system.[2]

The Dunnigan resolution was a long, rambling catchall. Its tone was plaintive, slightly incoherent. Apparently directed chiefly at the Board of Higher Education, the resolution referred to subversive activities only as one of numerous alleged deficiencies in the operation of the city schools. Without be-

[2] For the text of the Dunnigan resolution, see Appendix IV.

71

ing more specific, the resolution mentioned un-American activities, class and racial hatreds, indecent and immoral conditions which transgressed the rights of citizens and the ideals and principles of every citizen—Catholic, Protestant, or Jew. It charged the administration of the schools with using coercive methods in intimidating educators to the point where they were forced to withdraw; abuses of academic freedom were also alleged.

The Dunnigan resolution was referred to the Senate Finance Committee and was not reported out, but it produced action. On March 26, the Assembly approved the Rapp resolution which proposed a joint legislative committee to investigate the procedures and methods of allocating state moneys for public schools. This resolution was approved by the Senate the following day. By some behind-the-scenes negotiation, this resolution was recalled on March 29 and repassed by both chambers with the addition of a new subsection which broadened the committee's mandate. The text of the new subsection, the only part of the entire resolution which does not concern itself exclusively with financial matters, follows:

(i) The administration and conduct of the public school system of the City of New York, including the Board of Education and the Board of Higher Education; methods and subject matter of instruction; methods of appointments, removal and retirement of persons holding positions in the supervising, teaching, custodian and administrative staffs; the extent to which, if any, subversive activities may have been permitted to be carried on in the schools and colleges of such educational system; the practices and activities of the Municipal Civil Service Commission in the conduct of examinations, promulgation of lists and certification of appointments to positions under the supervision of the said Board of Education and Board of Higher Education.

The newly amended resolution was passed unanimously by the Assembly without debate. When it came before the Senate, there was considerable comment. Senator Dunnigan expressed approval of the new arrangement whereby Senator Frederic R. Coudert, Jr., the only Republican Senator from New York City, should become vice-chairman of the joint committee and take over this new function. His accompanying remarks give added point to the probability that at this time, at least insofar as he himself was concerned, the chief bogey was something other than communism, the single topic which was actually to absorb most of the committee's attention. Senator Dunnigan asserted that recent trends in education in New York City were "evidence of scholastic decadence," that the Russell appointment was typical of the "ungodly and un-American tradition which those in control of the school system in New York City are attempting to instill in the hearts and minds of the children and youth of the schools of the city." Declaring that it was a widely known fact that Russell's philosophy "debauched religion, the State and the family relationship," he concluded that the "attitude of the authority which insisted upon the appointment, despite great public opposition, is a matter of concern for the legislature."

The amended resolution received unanimous approval in the Senate amidst some speculation whether Governor Lehman would veto the item of $30,000 in the supplementary budget appropriated for the committee. Legislative comment indicated that in such an event the inquiry would proceed anyway because funds would be made available from the legislature's contingent fund. The Governor approved the item without comment, April 29, 1940, and the way was cleared for the inquiry to proceed. At the outset, reaction to the forthcoming investigation was mixed. The Teachers Union and the College Teachers Union quickly branded the committee as a front for real-estate interests and other selfish groups intent upon cutting educational budgets. Others, less unfriendly, also revealed their belief that the financial phases of the legislative directive constituted the important issue. James Marshall, president of the Board of Education of New York City, gave voice to this view when he observed, "I have complete confidence in Senator Coudert. My only hope is that the Legislature gets a competent staff to study finances and educational needs of the schools." He declined to comment on the phase of the investigation relating to subversive activities in the schools.

A *New York Times* editorial expressed a similar view. After commenting briefly on the forthcoming inquiry into subversive activities in the schools, the editorial continued, "The second and more important section of the inquiry is long overdue," in reference to the investigation of state aid to education. Other observers followed the action of the legislature with a note of uneasiness, however, and wondered whether teachers and the schools were in for an ordeal. In a letter to the *New York Times,* the venerable and respected John Dewey, representing the Committee for Cultural Freedom, expressed the fears engendered by such an investigation and stipulated the safeguards which could prevent it from becoming an instrument of oppression rather than of inquiry. He linked together the Rapp-Coudert and the Dies investigations: "Ostensibly in the public interest, both of these announcements have a vagueness about them that gives rise to legitimate apprehension on the part of progressive educators and experienced observers." He believed, however, that there could be no objection to such an investigation, "provided, that in line with the best educational practice, the investigation has a clear-cut objective and that the investigators themselves are competent to pursue it without prejudice or favor."

The Investigators

Assemblyman Herbert A. Rapp, author of the original resolution calling for investigation of the allocation of state financial aid, was named chairman of the committee at the outset.

Senator Frederic R. Coudert, Jr., became vice-chairman and chairman of the special subcommittee to investigate subversive activities in New York City. After the first period of the committee's activity, Mr. Rapp took no part in the New York City investigation. None of the other eleven members of the entire committee, including the four who with Senator Coudert constituted the subcommittee, were influential forces in the work of the committee. These four subcommittee members, Senator John L. Buckley and Peter T. Farrell and Assemblymen John D. Bennett and Sheldon F. Wicks, were only occasionally present at the sessions of the committee.

Throughout the subcommittee's existence it was identified chiefly with a single name, that of its chairman, Senator Coudert. Accounts differ as to the reasons which led to Coudert's selection for this post, but even those who have been most highly critical admit that the choice was logical. Senator Coudert had been active in various matters affecting the schools over a period of years. In the previous session, as one of the sponsors of the Coudert-Crews bill, he had been instrumental in the enactment of legislation protecting tenure in the city colleges.

Other than Senator Coudert, the active persons in the inquiry were the members of a highly paid professional staff, chiefly lawyers. Paul Windels, a prominent New York attorney who had served for a time as corporation counsel under Mayor La Guardia, was chosen as counsel. Press comment generally hailed his appointment as a happy augury. The *New York Times* observed, "If further evidence were needed that State Senator Coudert's legislative committee to investigate the New York City schools does not propose a witch hunt, it was provided by the appointment of Paul Windels yesterday as the committee's counsel. . . . If there are subversive activities in the schools, he will find them, but we can trust him not to invent them. Senator Coudert and his colleagues have done

75

well and are to be congratulated on this important first step."
Mr. Windels named as his chief aide Phillip Haberman, Jr.,
who had served on the staff of Samuel Seabury during an earlier legislative investigation. A half-dozen additional lawyers
and investigators were employed throughout the committee's
existence. This is in marked contrast to the policy followed
by the abortive McNaboe inquiry, where the committee members attempted unsuccessfully to carry out the investigative
work themselves. It follows, of course, that the Coudert procedure was much more expensive.

The Committee's Record

The committee began its investigative work about the first
of September, 1940. Beginning on December 2, it held public
hearings for three days. Further public hearings were held
from March through June, 1941. As will be explained later,
the committee encountered marked resistance in the form of
legal questions concerning its powers, and its work did not
progress rapidly. Early in January it became clear that a report
could not be rendered by February 1, 1941, the date stipulated
in the resolution. Senator Coudert's request for an extension
of time and clarification of powers was readily granted. The
time extension until March 15, 1942, was once more extended
to June 1, 1942. The committee's final report, dated February
11, 1942, was actually released on April 23, 1942.

It is impossible to state precisely how much the committee
spent. The original appropriation of $30,000 was supple-
mented by subsequent grants of $45,000 on January 21, 1941,
$100,000 on May 4, 1941, and $44,000 on May 24, 1941. A
further appropriation of $50,000 was made in March, 1942. In
the case of the first and last of these grants, facts are not available to show how much went to inquiries other than the one
here discussed. Part of the original $30,000 was absorbed by
the financial studies of the parent committee. From March,

1942, until February, 1947, the Rapp-Coudert committee, under the new designation of the Joint Legislative Committee on the State Educational System, carried on extensive studies of state educational finance and administration. Just where the dividing line on expenditures of these various enterprises should be drawn is a matter hidden deeply in the accounts of the state comptroller. If the cost of the investigation of subversive activities in New York during 1940–1941 is placed at approximately $250,000, the figure is probably not wide of the mark.

Three reports were issued by the committee. The first of these, *Legislative Document* (1941), No. 54, was released on March 24, 1941. This seventy-six-page report deals chiefly with the financial phase of the committee's work; Part II, comprising seventeen pages, is devoted to the subcommittee on subversive activities. On December 1, 1941, the subcommittee issued its *Interim Report and Conclusions of the New York City Subcommittee Relative to Subversive Activity among Students in the Public High Schools and Colleges in the City of New York,* 132 pages. Its final report, dated February 11, 1942, was actually released on April 23, *Legislative Document* (1942), No. 49, 394 pages. A number of other reports were issued by the Rapp-Coudert committee between 1942 and 1947. While all of these reports deal with the state educational system and some of them specifically with the schools and colleges of New York City, none are concerned with the subject of this report, subversive activities; hence, they are excluded from consideration.

As a matter of fact, the work of the Coudert subcommittee was terminated rather than completed. The invasion of the Soviet Union by Hitler in June, 1941, transformed the entire political situation. For the moment, American-Russian relations became more friendly; furthermore, attention shifted from the domestic to the foreign front. The entry into military service of many persons close to the investigation, including several members of the staff and some of those who were being investigated, served further to deprive the inquiry of the interest it had formerly held. One can only speculate what would have been the ultimate result if the war had not intervened.

The next section of this report will attempt to give a detailed account of the inquiry as it developed in order to throw into relief the attitudes of the committee, the assumptions upon which it acted, its procedures, problems, and methods of meeting them. It will also be necessary to describe the activities of those groups and individuals who opposed the committee's efforts. After this has been done, an effort will be made to appraise the work of the committee.

From the outset, the Joint Committee functioned in two separate groups. The full committee with its own separate professional staff attacked state-wide educational problems. Its report of March 24, 1941, recommended specific legislation covering state aid, consolidation of school districts, and construction of school buildings in central school districts. After January 14, 1941, the committee as a whole ceased to function; it remained inactive until, by a resolution adopted March 23, 1942, it was redesignated the Joint Legislative Committee on the State Education System. By that time the subversive activities investigation had been discontinued; thereafter, the committee, still called the Rapp-Coudert committee, returned to its original assignment: state financial aid to education. Between 1942 and 1947, when it was dissolved, the committee issued a number of valuable technical reports. Many of its recommendations have already been enacted into law; others are still live issues.

During its later period the committee functioned exclusively through professional research staffs. Experts with established reputations in educational administration were engaged to recruit appropriate technical help and conduct the investigation through research rather than inquisitorial methods. At this point the investigation dropped out of the headlines so completely that the general public was not even aware that the committee continued to function. Part of the striking change was attributable, no doubt, to the fact that educational costs hold less press appeal than Communist teachers, but the new procedures were also instrumental in contributing to a more decorous atmosphere.

As the Coudert subcommittee got under way, it made several policy decisions covering the scope of its inquiries and the rules of procedure under which it would operate. Despite the fact that subsection (i) included virtually all phases of school administration in New York City, including such matters as methods and subject matter of instruction and all phases of personnel, the committee decided to concentrate upon the single topic of subversive activities. Actually, in the closing days of its existence, the committee did extend its inquiry to include alleged abuses in letting of contracts for student chemistry kits and a brief excursion into the events surrounding the exits of Presidents Robinson and Colligan. These matters were clearly subsidiary, however; that they were incidental is evidenced by the eighteen pages which they receive in a 394-page report.

Committee Intentions and Objectives

A haze of contradictory assertions obscures the facts concerning the original intentions of the Coudert subcommittee. High ranking, responsible members of the committee staff place great emphasis upon two points. They point out first that the original intention of Senator Coudert when he accepted the chairmanship of the subcommittee on New York City was to concentrate upon school finances. This, they contend, continued to be his primary concern as the committee was organized and began its preliminary work. The second point stressed is that the decision to look into subversive activities came about as a result of a staff recommendation to Senator Coudert and grew directly out of representations made to the staff by persons actively interested in the New York City school system. Staff members insist that a change in emphasis occurred between the time the subcommittee was created and the time it actually began active investigative work and that this shift was dictated by the presentation of such compelling evidence that they could not ignore it.

A sharply contradictory point of view is taken by the Teachers Union and those closely associated with it. At the time the creation of the subcommittee was announced and long before the actual investigation had gotten under way, the Teachers Union through its legislative representative, its president, and other official spokesmen charged that Senator Coudert and his associates would employ Red-baiting tactics as a screen for the real objective of budget cutting.

Press accounts announcing the creation of the subcommittee linked together the fact of Senator Coudert's association with it and the assumption that its main assignment was to look into subversive activities. Whatever the original intentions of Senator Coudert, his associates, and staff, press reports indicate that contemporary observers took it for granted that subversive activities—whatever that ominously vague term might mean—were to be the principal item on the subcommittee's agenda.

Perhaps it is unnecessary to speculate over the committee's original intent and whether its subsequent concentration upon assertedly Communist schoolteachers was accidental or deliberate. The incident does underline one aspect of the investigation that was particularly unfortunate and should certainly be avoided in the future. The fact that the authorizing resolution combined two objectives, financial conditions and subversive activities, made inevitable the unnecessary complications that resulted.

Legislative investigations of controversial subjects, for reasons which are not difficult to understand, often arouse extremes of reaction, not only among those placed under scrutiny but on the part of the general observer as well. Any policy or practice which needlessly exacerbates controversy, thereby inviting reciprocally immoderate tendencies from the investigator and those investigated, must be adjudged a bad policy. The unnecessary joining together of a financial survey and a disciplinary issue intensified fear and confusion and furnished at least a plausible pretext for expressions of suspicion. The question of Senator Coudert's good faith—a point which ran as a recurrent strain throughout the entire investigation—was precipitated through the unwise decision to join together two unrelated and incompatible subjects: finance and subversive activities.

It may be well to pause at this point to comment upon Mr. Coudert's part in the investigation which bore his name. As related earlier, his selection as chairman of the New York City subcommittee of the Rapp committee had been explained by persons close to the situation on the grounds that he was the only Republican member of the Senate from New York City, but there were other reasons. For several years prior to the creation of the committee, he had been more active than most of his Senate colleagues in legislation affecting the schools; he had been the sponsor of a number of rather major pieces of legislation on educational matters. During the period of the investigation Senator Coudert was pictured as an enemy of the schools, but his record in the legislature simply cannot be squared with this assertion.[3]

Throughout the life of the New York City subcommittee,

[3] The following extract from an unpublished report prepared by the then chairman of the New York Committee on Academic Freedom of the American Civil Liberties Union is pertinent in this connection:

Senator Coudert remained actively associated with the work carried on, but his relationship to its everyday work, hence to many of the decisions on policy and procedure, was not quite what it appeared. As chairman of the subcommittee, Mr. Coudert believed that the only way for it to function effectively was to select the best counsel and professional staff obtainable and then allow them free hand to do their job. He steadfastly adhered to this plan. The staff consulted him at all times, but the investigation as planned and executed was its own handiwork, not that of the committee or its chairman. At some points during the public hearings Senator Coudert participated actively in the questioning of witnesses. Even here, however, his role was distinctly minor. He chose, rather, to serve as the committee's spokesman before the legislature and the general public. At all times he defended the staff in its work and accepted full responsibility for what it did.

Committee Procedures Evoke Criticism

As the investigation got under way, Paul Windels issued a statement asking for co-operation and inviting the public to give information to the committee.[4] He promised that indi-

---

"It may be of interest to readers of this report to know that Senator Coudert, who was the chairman of the subcommittee which operated in New York City under the general Rapp-Coudert Committee, is the same Senator Coudert who, at the request of the faculties of the city colleges, sponsored the tenure law in the Senate of the State of New York, and secured for it the unanimous vote of the New York State Senate. Had it not been for the fact that this law was on the statute books of New York State (certainly in large part due to the highly competent work of Senator Coudert in assisting the faculties of the city colleges to get the protection of a state tenure law) the Board of Higher Education of New York City could have dismissed without so much as a hearing any members of the staff considered guilty of misconduct. It is certainly true that the accused members of the staffs of the New York City Colleges had more protection under the Coudert-Crews tenure law than is enjoyed by the staffs of most other colleges and universities in the United States" (J. M. O'Neill, "State Legislatures and Higher Education" [1945]).

4 *New York Times,* August 18, 1940, p. 5.

viduals who wished to appear before the committee could do so in private and that their disclosures would remain confidential. The committee felt that all interests would be best served by using the private interview as the initial method of eliciting information. Ordinarily these interviews were conducted by one or more members of the staff without administering an oath. If the statements of the individual concerned seemed to warrant recording, a member of the committee would attend and administer an oath and a stenotypist would take down the witness' testimony. Only after a person had been thus interrogated privately was he placed upon the stand in public hearings. The single exception to this procedure produced unfortunate results and will be noted later.

The extensive use of the private hearing procedure is illustrated in the following figures: in public hearings the committee heard 88 witnesses who gave 2,297 pages of testimony; in private hearings the committee interrogated 503 witnesses who gave 13,340 pages of testimony. More than two hundred additional persons were interviewed but were not sworn. It is thus seen that the major portion of the committee's work was not carried on in the full glare of publicity.

The committee contends that its motives in following this procedure were inspired wholly by the desire to avoid smearing innocent people by the disclosure of allegations which had not been verified. In support of its position it asserts that scores of names of alleged Communists were supplied by those who gave private testimony. Under its practices, no person would be named publicly unless his identification as a member of the Communist Party had been attested to by at least two witnesses or unless other corroborative evidence was available.

The committee also justifies its private-public hearing procedure on the ground that only in this way could orderly, fruitful proceedings be assured. Otherwise, time would be frittered away on irresponsible, self-seeking witnesses who would lower the dignity and destroy the effectiveness of the inquiry. Finally, the committee insists that only by the private hearing procedure could the best interests of students be preserved:

> Evidence concerning the actual operations of the Communist Youth movement in the city schools and colleges has been obtained through the testimony of students who were not afraid to tell the truth. Although no promises were made to withhold their names from public disclosure, we are of the opinion that their identities should be shielded. Revealing them would serve no useful purpose.
>
> It has been deemed the wiser course, therefore, not to call these young people at public hearings but to have prepared by counsel a strictly factual summary of the evidence given in the private hearings, fully quoting testimony without revealing in the case of students the names of the witnesses who gave it.[5]

The technique of the private hearing has something to be said in its favor. Certainly, anyone who has followed some of the unrehearsed sessions of our congressional committees, investigatory or otherwise, would concede that there is much to be gained by establishing a satisfactory screening procedure.

Exponents of the private hearing procedure contend that no other instrumentality can produce comparable results during the preliminary or exploratory stages of an investigation. Because of the necessity of following up all manner of leads in order to determine which are worthy of extensive attention, the investigating staff frequently becomes the recipient of tip-offs and allegations which range all the way from outright falsehoods through unsubstantiated rumors to highly credible information. Only by keeping every statement within the confines of the committee until its credibility has been confirmed can the committee inform itself, yet protect innocent people. Advocates of the use of the private hearing admit that every

[5] New York City Subcommittee, *Interim Report,* p. 4.

thing depends upon the good will and good judgment of those who are conducting the investigation. No other safeguards are provided. If the staff is able and responsible, none are needed; if the staff is not, no amount of protection will prevent abuse.

Those who defend the private interview and private hearings stress the importance of maintaining the confidential character of the information adduced. It should not be regarded as part of the committee's findings, hence available for public inspection. Rather, it is part of the investigatory equipment to be used in the development of the information which the committee is directed to obtain. When it has served its purpose and the information has been made public either through the medium of public hearings or in the final report, the private hearing data should be destroyed. This was the procedure employed by Samuel Seabury in the investigation of New York City government and it was the procedure adopted by the Coudert committee.

In the case of the Coudert committee, however, the preliminary private hearings were conducted in such a way as to leave the committee vulnerable to attack whether or not the procedure was actually such as to justify attack. First of all, the committee refused to permit a witness to be accompanied by counsel; second, he could not obtain a copy of his statement; third, he was questioned in the presence of only a single member of the committee, and frequently no committee member at all would be present during the interrogation. In fact, the committee member appeared only long enough to administer the oath; then he retired, leaving the witness with one or more members of the staff and a stenotypist.

It is readily conceded that witnesses at legislative hearings, whether formal or informal, have no positive right to be accompanied by counsel. But is there not at least a strongly persuasive argument for the utmost leniency on the part of the investigating committee so long as the effectiveness of its procedures is not impaired? What does it have to lose by extending voluntarily a courtesy which clearly cannot be exacted as a right? Until more evidence than now seems to exist is accumulated to prove that any concession to the amenities handicaps a committee in achieving its ends, experiments along this line should be encouraged.

Those who question the validity of the plea for admitting counsel to such hearings point out that a witness appearing before a grand jury investigation is not extended the privilege of being accompanied by a professional adviser. The witness before a legislative committee, so it is argued, is likewise not a party to the proceeding, hence not entitled to counsel. The analogy is not convincing for two reasons. In the first place, many of the persons summoned before the Rapp-Coudert committee were parties to the proceeding in the very real sense that their jobs were under jeopardy. If the issue of being a party to the proceedings is a crucial one, then denial of counsel actually infringed the witnesses' rights. A second reason why grand jury procedure does not suggest itself as a compelling precedent for a legislative hearing lies in the differences in atmosphere, procedure, attitude in the two proceedings. The very nature of the personnel—both lay (jury or legislators) and professional (prosecuting attorney or committee counsel)—is such that the rights of the witness are more likely to be protected in the grand jury hearing. The annals of investigating committee proceedings reveal a record of irregularity completely unapproached by grand jury hearings.

The committee's refusal to supply a witness with a copy of his testimony seemingly had no practical justification. In the interest of ordinary accuracy, the purposes of the committee would have been furthered, and the witness could have the assurance that he had not been misunderstood or inaccurately recorded. Furthermore, the committee would have removed one of the most embarrassing charges against it. Many persons who were generally sympathetic to the committee and disposed to support it against the unrestrained attack which emanated from some quarters, were puzzled and distressed by this regulation. If the refusal had been based on expense or any other known ground, the necessity for it could have been appraised. As matters stood, the committee's decision appeared in the light of a cavalier discourtesy to the interested parties.

The committee's position was further weakened because after some delay it permitted the person being interrogated to take notes. Some witnesses carried this to the point of writing down verbatim all questions asked them and their answers thereto. Under these conditions it was impossible to plead the danger of disclosure as the justification for refusal to supply a transcript of testimony; yet the committee laid itself open to the charge of star chamber tactics. Had it yielded on this point, it is difficult to see how its work would have been impaired, and it would have avoided a criticism that created serious misgivings in the minds of impartial observers.[6]

Early in its investigation the committee issued subpoenas to a large number of Brooklyn College instructors requesting their appearance at private hearings. On the advice of legal counsel, twenty-five of this group declined to appear because they questioned the legality of the private hearing procedure. An action requesting a declaratory judgment was instituted in the New York State Supreme Court to determine whether the committee had authority to proceed in this manner. Pend-

[6] On January 29, 1941, in a long memorandum to the Rapp-Coudert committee, the New York City Committee and the Committee on Academic Freedom, both subsidiaries of the American Civil Liberties Union, offered several procedural recommendations. On the specific point of private hearings the memorandum stated, "But on grounds of public policy we urge that a stenographic record be taken of such preliminary examinations and that an opportunity be given the witness to correct stenographer's errors. This is the method commonly adopted by congressional investigating committees, including even the Dies Committee. It prevents the misuse even of informal testimony."

ing judicial determination of this point, the members of the group reiterated their unwillingness to appear.

At the termination of open hearings on December 4, Committee Counsel Paul Windels presented the names of those who had refused to testify at private hearings. The committee directed him to institute contempt proceedings with instructions to permit any of the group to purge themselves voluntarily if they chose to appear.

The committee interpreted this group's action as a Communist-inspired tactic to thwart progress by raising all manner of technical issues to block the inquiry at every turn. "During the first five months of the investigation, our time was occupied and our energies diverted by litigation with persons seeking to obstruct the inquiry." [7]

As will be related later, the Teachers Union lost no opportunity to attack the committee by impugning its motives and distorting its methods, but the committee was not justified in imputing obstructive motives to all who resisted its procedures. An excerpt from a letter which the twenty-five Brooklyn College instructors sent to Chairman Ordway Tead of the Board of Higher Education in explanation of their position underlines this point. After explaining that they had refused to testify at private hearings at which Senator Coudert was the only member of the committee present, the letter continues:

Witnesses who submitted to testify before Mr. Coudert found out that they had waived the right to have any legislator present, for it became Mr. Coudert's practice to leave the private hearing room after swearing the witness. Questioned by numerous assistant counsel, the witness learned that no transcript of his own answers would be available to him. The record could be had only by Mr. Coudert and his counsel. In consequence, even Senator Coudert's witness, Dr. Grebanier, later found it necessary to deny under oath at the public hearing that he had given the testimony

[7] *Final Report,* Legislative Document (1942), No. 49, p. 6.

attributed to him upon the private hearing minutes. . . . Naturally the question of law can be decided authoritatively by the courts alone. As soon as such decision is made, and counsel tells us what it is, we are going to comply with it. We want to know how far it is our duty to submit to Mr. Coudert's method.[8]

At least half of the signers of this letter were persons who had no connection with the alleged Communist activities then under investigation. They could not be fairly accused of a conspiracy to balk the committee; rather, they were sincerely disturbed by the potentialities of a procedure which had no safeguards against error or abuse. The committee refused to concede to these persons the same concern for fair play which it arrogated to itself. In its final report it comments upon the incident as follows:

In November, 1940, the Committee succeeded in obtaining at its private hearings testimony concerning the membership of several members of the faculty of Brooklyn College in a Communist Party unit at that college. Twenty teachers, including the individuals referred to, were duly subpoenaed to testify at the private hearings. These twenty teachers, using a carefully prepared legalistic formula, in which they had been rehearsed by the Teachers Union, refused to make any answers to the questions which were put at the hearings.[9]

It seems clear that the committee, unconscious of any desire to abuse its power and convinced of the justice of its position and the soundness of its legal authority, attributed to ulterior design what was in reality honest doubt on the part of at least some of the signers.

The committee's attitude in this instance was consistent with a tendency which unfortunately was manifest throughout

[8] Letter dated December 16, 1940, in files of Board of Higher Education. See below, p. 156.

[9] *Final Report*, p. 234.

its proceedings. All persons who were interested in the committee's work were identified by it as either friend or foe. Opposition to its methods or policies was viewed as carefully contrived obstructionism. Through its unwillingness to credit the sincerity of any of its critics, the committee sealed itself off from the constructive comment that might otherwise have saved it from mistakes.

In its insistence that the Brooklyn staff members appear at private hearings on its own terms, the committee chose to stand upon its legal rights and was fully supported in the courts. One doubts that the victory was worth the price. Not one of the points which caused so much criticism—honest and otherwise—bore vitally upon the committee's capacity to discharge its function. In each instance it could have yielded, yet gained the information it sought. In only a single respect would yielding have increased the inconvenience to which the committee was put. More time on the part of the members of the investigating committee would have been required if they were to be present during private hearings. This does not seem an unreasonable cost when the subject was one that so vitally affected those summoned before the committee. However, the point of having committee members present would have been much less important if the witness had been protected by receiving a transcript of his testimony.

The committee has failed to give a satisfying reason for its failure to make an adjustment in its procedures to mollify its critics. Its explanation is that this was not a criminal proceeding, that the person was charged with no crime, that legislative investigating committees were not obligated to provide the safeguards so earnestly sought. All of these points are conceded, but they do not make clear what the committee would have lost by extending full courtesy and consideration to those appearing before it. Such liberal interpretation of its procedural obligations would have been eminently appropriate for a committee which was attempting to protect democratic institutions.

The Committee and the Teachers Union

Another decision early in the inquiry produced unfortunate repercussions at a time when interested nonparticipants were attempting to think their way through the complexities of the investigation and arrive at reasoned conclusions. In one of its earliest moves the committee raised in many minds serious questions as to its motives and its judgment when it decided to force the Teachers Union to reveal its membership lists. After its request to the officers of the Teachers Union for the membership lists had been refused, the committee resorted to a *subpoena duces tecum* in order to compel their delivery. Again there was no real question of the committee's power. After considerable delay occasioned by successive appeals, the New York Court of Appeals sustained the subpoena and the membership lists were surrendered. The committee hailed the decision as a victory, but there is ground for believing that the incident as a whole was detrimental to the committee. The entire membership list issue deserves further examination because it effectively illustrates the complex forces generated in an investigation of so elusive an element as subversive activities.

Evidence presented at some of the early private hearings coupled with research into the publications then being distributed in considerable volume convinced the committee that the Communist Party dominated the Teachers Union and the College Teachers Union. In order to verify its assumption and supplement its list of alleged members of the Communist Party, the committee decided that it should scrutinize the membership rolls of the unions.

It has never been made clear just how the possession of these lists was supposed to aid the committee. The arguments offered by Mr. Windels in his several appearances at judicial proceedings skirted the issue of utility and concentrated upon the question of power. In the light of the committee's subsequent disclosures it now seems clear that little use was made of the lists—for the simple reason that they yielded no information which the committee did not already have. The lists did not show any political affiliation because under union rules such information was not requested from members. Inasmuch as all active members of the union were already well known, the union lists could add nothing to the committee's information.

The only possibility that remained, therefore, in the eyes of many observers, was that under the guise of hunting for Communists the committee was seeking to undermine the unions by making public their membership. Many persons had joined the teachers' unions just as others had joined carpenters' unions and miners' unions—to increase their bargaining power—but they hesitated to disclose their affiliation because of fear that they might be retaliated against by those out of sympathy with employee organizations. Such timidity may be dismissed as unjustified, therefore unworthy of consideration as a reason for preserving the secrecy of membership lists. The fact still remains that union membership has in the past and continues today to be frowned upon in some quarters. Under such conditions the strength of a union's recruiting program may depend directly upon its ability to preserve the anonymity of its members.

Incidentally, both federal and state statutes protect carpenters and miners against discrimination because of their union membership. By contrast, no statute protects a teacher against the hostility which his union membership may engender.

Many persons who held no brief for communism and who were generally in sympathy with the Coudert committee felt compelled to protest this move. Professor George S. Counts, president of the American Federation of Teachers, the parent organization with which the local union was affiliated, stated:

> The national office of the American Federation of Teachers is unalterably opposed to the opening of membership lists of a voluntary organization to the authorities of government unless this is done in such a way as to safeguard completely the rights of all persons involved. It is the beginning of a road which may lead to government control of all unions and the end of the free labor movement in America.[10]

Professor Counts certainly could not be regarded as a sympathizer with communism or a special pleader for the local unions. For more than a year preceding this statement, he had been under heavy attack from the local organizations. The pages of the *New York Teacher,* the monthly journal of Local No. 5, the union of New York City public school teachers, reveal little identity of interest or viewpoint between Counts and local union leaders.

In a letter dated October 22, 1940, Osmond K. Fraenkel and Florina Lasker of the American Civil Liberties Union protested to Paul Windels, counsel of the Coudert committee, that his action in subpoenaing the lists was both unwise and unnecessary. After pointing out that the committee already had the complete list of teachers of the city schools and had talked with the union officers and seen its records, the letter said further action was not only unwarranted but would link the Teachers Union and the Communist Party to the detriment of labor union activity. The letter concluded that resort to subpoena to force delivery of the membership lists would "coerce and intimidate teachers from engaging in labor union activity for fear that such membership will prejudice their rights and even their jobs."

The membership lists issue was unfortunate; it needlessly

10 *New York Times,* October 16, 1940, p. 25.

complicated a situation already full of controversy without promoting materially the interests of the committee. If the matter had been dropped when resistance occurred, the whole thing would quickly have fallen from sight. But the committee chose to interpret union resistance as a threat to its power and prestige. It fought the point through the Court of Appeals, where its power to subpoena the lists was upheld by a unanimous decision.[11]

The events surrounding the action of the committee, once the court had sustained it, suggest that if the strategy of the opposition had been to provoke the committee into hasty, ill-considered action which would reflect adversely upon its fairness and moderation, the committee had played right into its hands.

The Court of Appeals announced its decision in Albany on Thursday, January 23. On Friday the committee delivered to Charles J. Hendley, Teachers Union president, a letter informing him that an arrest order had been signed and asking whether he would surrender the lists. Hendley replied that he desired to consult his attorney, whereupon the sheriff attempted to serve the arrest warrant the following morning. These facts were made known in a statement released by Mr. Windels on Saturday, January 25.[12] Actually, the full text of the Court of Appeals decision did not become available until Monday. Technically Mr. Hendley was on sound ground in withholding his compliance until the decision had been formally filed in New York County. His delay in responding to the committee's request could irritate but not otherwise injure its members.

Mr. Windels permitted himself to be goaded into retaliatory action. His statement for the press on Saturday smacked of Communist tactics because it conveyed a false impression that could hardly have been inadvertent. No significant aspect of

---

[11] *In the Matter of Hendley*, 285 N.Y. 1 (1941).
[12] *New York Times*, January 26, 1941, p. 1.

the committee's work could have been seriously disrupted by a delay of twenty-four or forty-eight hours. Had the union then failed to comply with the decision, the burden would have rested squarely upon it. As it was, the premature action of Mr. Windels lent considerable plausibility to the union charge that orderly procedures could no longer be expected.

Upon two later occasions the Coudert committee showed that it had not changed its mind about the question of membership lists. On February 11, 1941, it subpoenaed the lists of the College Teachers Union and upon the refusal of union officers to surrender the list, contempt proceedings were instituted.[13] Decision of the union officers to comply resulted in the withdrawal of the contempt action. In July of the same year the Coudert committee requested the American Student Union to surrender its lists. The latter action seemed particularly questionable in view of the nature of the organization and its lack of relationship to the school system. The committee had defended its right to examine the union lists on the ground that labor unions are now legally established institutions and as such no longer should enjoy the right to withhold their membership from the public, especially of a legislative committee responsible to the public. But this argument could not be applied to a student organization.

The committee's record on the membership list issue does not excite admiration. Before leaving the subject, however, one point on the favorable side of the ledger should be mentioned. At least part of the opposition to the committee's demand for the union lists stemmed from the assumption that they would be made public. Mr. Windels insisted from the beginning that the committee intended to hold membership information in confidence, but his assurances were not given much weight by his critics. To his great credit the lists were never made public.

13 *Ibid.*, February 12, 1941, p. 23.

The Committee's Sources of Information

Another policy decision which had far-reaching effects upon the entire inquiry occurred when the committee decided to build its case primarily upon the testimony of a single key witness. Like the decision to concentrate on subversive activities, it was a staff decision and came about more through adventitious circumstances than from design. When the staff decided to look first for evidence of subversive activity, it knew nothing about the subject and had little interest in it. Early efforts to obtain information were largely abortive because those interviewed simply refused to divulge any information. Quite by chance, the committee staff stumbled upon certain members of the college faculties who had at one time been members of the Communist Party. In the earlier instances, the erratic character of the witnesses prevented the staff from making great use of this testimony because of the impossibility of corroborating it. In fact, it soon became apparent that while the general outline of this early testimony was substantially correct, many of the details were sufficiently garbled to throw serious doubt upon the credibility of any specific point except those which could be verified from other sources.

Later in the inquiry, William Canning, a former member of the Communist unit at City College, consented after considerable reluctance to co-operate with the investigating staff. He had been a member of the Communist Party for several years during which he had taken an active part in many of its activities. In addition, he had served for some months as party treasurer, a post which had obligated him to collect dues from his City College colleagues who were also in the party. Three other members of the City College staff who had been members of the party for shorter periods were able to corroborate much of his testimony. Further corroboration was obtained from outside sources and from written records. The result was that while by no means every point of testimony offered by the committee witnesses was verified, it could be cross-checked at sufficient places to guarantee a degree of accuracy completely lacking in the earlier testimony.

By carefully screening the official literature of the Communist Party, the committee staff established a hypothesis as to the party's objectives and operating procedures on the college campus. Then with the factual information in its possession it constructed its case as to what was actually taking place. This procedure, while undoubtedly accurate in major outline and in many details, had serious shortcomings. In the first place, it could and undoubtedly did err in particular instances. Some of the persons named by the key witness were indubitably members of the Communist Party; others probably were not. At least, even at this late date, available information suggests strongly that some names had been erroneously included in the list of alleged party members. The key witness was engaged actively in the work of at least three additional organizations at the time of his party membership. Several of the persons named by him as fellow party members were also fellow members in the Instructional Staff Association, the Anti-fascist Association, and the College Teachers Union, all of which held numerous meetings throughout this period. It is well known, of course, that many of the members of these organizations were completely out of sympathy with the Communist Party.

There is little doubt that some of the persons identified as Communist associates of the witness were actually colleagues in one or more of the other groups. Even though the committee made some effort to confirm the party affiliation of each person before his or her name was made public during the public hearings, it seems certain that some mistakes were made. In view of the serious consequences which would almost inevitably follow upon such public disclosure, the committee was not sufficiently thorough in setting up adequate safeguards against error. Its explanation that disclosure constituted neither indictment nor conviction and that any mistakes could be rectified by the person falsely accused, hardly reflects the scrupulous concern for individual rights that should accompany every legislative investigation.

To the charge that the committee permitted individuals to be tabbed publicly as Communists without exercising proper care to verify its information, the official answer was that the individuals so named had been given an opportunity to present their case in private hearings. If, through failure to appear or refusal to answer questions, the accused had declined to aid the committee in its search for the true facts, he could not later complain of committee negligence. Studied resistance, concerted refusal to answer committee questions, characterized the behavior of some of the teachers who were summoned before the committee. It had little encouragement in its efforts to preserve the amenities. No gesture of appreciation came from those being investigated, and progress was not such as to indicate that patience was paying off. Nevertheless, the moral position of the committee was strong so long as it could continue to report that every person under suspicion had been given an opportunity to tell his side of the story before his name had been made public.

It is particularly disquieting to learn that even this minimal precaution was not observed in at least some cases. A member of the staff of City College whom the committee named as a Communist stated that he had not been accorded an opportunity to appear at a private session. He continued:

If this committee had questioned me at the private hearings about Mr. Canning's statements concerning me, I could have established their falsity at that time. If the Committee had done this instead of, through its Counsel, encouraging Mr. Canning to introduce my name by asking him at public hearings of this Committee: "How about the Mathematics Department? Was there an instructor there?" the College as well as I and my family would have been spared the injury that has come from irresponsible testimony about me at your public hearings and from the resulting newspaper publicity.[14]

This disturbing disclosure elicited no denial or explanation from the committee. The individual in question was never tried or removed by the college authorities. He remains today a member of the City College faculty, so he must have been falsely or erroneously named; but his innocence was not enough to protect him from this humiliating experience.

In specific instances individuals identified as Communists by the key committee witness were able to point out discrepancies in certain portions of his testimony. It is reasonable to assume that even though he was a witness of exceptional ability and could recapitulate factual detail with an unusual degree of accuracy, he was not infallible. An example of one such instance will illustrate. One person was named by the committee's key witness and confirmed by another committee witness, but neither witness could link him with any specific party activity. There was absolutely no detail, simply the statement that they had seen him at Communist meetings.

Both witnesses had earlier testified that the party required all of its members to be active; they spoke of instances where members were rebuked for inactivity. Neither witness could recall this individual's having been admonished, yet they were unable to point to any activity in which he had been engaged. Two further bits of contradictory evidence were available. The accused was on record as having publicly taken positions contrary to the party line. The committee witness who had at

14 New York City Subcommittee, *Public Hearings*, p. 1350.

one time served as party treasurer could not recall ever having received party dues from the accused. In addition to all this, when the key witness named the accused as a party member, he did not give his name correctly: he committed the same error that occurred in the City College catalogue. It seems likely that the committee witness had merely taken the City College catalogue and gone down the lists checking those whom he thought he remembered having seen at party meetings. Among the threescore named, some errors crept in.

In many cases his selections were correct because he had ample corroborative data. His error was no doubt an innocent one—a trick of memory which every one knows frequently occurs. In the instance just related the victim of error feels sure there was no motive in naming him falsely. He believes that it was simply a case of confused association, that his presence at some of the other organizations in which both were members had been mistakenly recollected as a party function. Unlike this respondent, some of those named by the committee witness did impute deliberate vindictive intent. The evidence is not full enough to justify a conclusion on this point, but it seems minor for present purposes. The important fact is that irrespective of motive, inaccuracies were present in the testimony of the committee's witnesses; nevertheless, there was a persistent tendency to accept without reservation whatever they said. It should be emphasized that the single instance of inaccuracy reported is not untypical. At least half a dozen other examples could be cited.

When the committee found that its informants were guilty of inaccuracies in specific instances, it erred in not double-checking every case before letting it be made public. The record shows such a close relationship between the public naming of a person, his appearance before the committee in public hearing, and his suspension by the educational authorities that, despite the protestations of the committee to the contrary, the act of naming him publicly as an alleged member of the Communist Party came very close to being both an indictment and a punishment.

Committee Attitudes

Certain procedural practices of the committee bear closely upon the matter just discussed because they tend to reflect something of the mental set of the committee and its staff, and also because they determine to a large degree the procedural remedies open to anyone named by the committee's informants as alleged members of the Communist Party. In the first place, when fifty-odd City College employees were publicly named as Communists, Senator Coudert gave them assurance that each of them would be granted an opportunity to appear before the committee publicly for the purpose of replying to the charges. He instructed all those who wished to appear to make a formal application in writing. These instructions were issued on March 7, 1941. Without delay those named filed their written requests for a public hearing. These letters were not acknowledged by the committee or its staff, but beginning approximately three weeks later the individuals concerned were served with subpoenas directing them to appear for a public hearing upon a stated day.

From conversations with a number of persons who underwent this experience, at least some of whom present a strong likelihood of having been innocent victims of confused identification, it seems clear that, unwitting though it may have been, the committee's action was unnecessarily harsh and unfair. In commenting upon the committee's employment of the subpoena, associate counsel for the committee observed, "It seems immaterial whether they were notified to appear by subpoena or by any other method available to the committee." [15] To an experienced attorney the point may have seemed

[15] *Papers on Appeal, Withrow et al. v. Joint Legislative Committee*, p. 37.

minor, but to educators falsely charged with conduct regarded as grounds for removal from employment it was far from reassuring to receive no acknowledgement of their initial request for a hearing and then some weeks later to be summoned by subpoena to appear. The committee had gone out of its way to convey to the individuals concerned, to their friends, and to that portion of the public which was in touch with proceedings the impression that it had already arrived at its own verdict of guilty. Otherwise, why accord these persons the kind of treatment usually reserved for those who are unwilling to appear except under compulsion?

Counsel for the Teachers Union subsequently brought suit to vacate the subpoenas of some of his clients. Among other grounds, he alleged that the strategy of the committee called for the use of the subpoena as part of a procedure which expedited the suspension of persons named as Communists. In support of his contention, he produced records to show that in the cases already heard there had been a direct time sequence between appearance at a public hearing of the committee and suspension by the educational authorities. Whether or not this latter point was part of a deliberate and conscious plan, the procedure of the committee does suggest strongly an attitude unsympathetic to those under investigation. It savors more of prosecution than of investigation, even though the protestations of the committee were entirely to the contrary. Other aspects of the public hearing procedures cast further light upon this point.

Counsel Paul Windels opened the public hearings by laying down the rules of procedure. Witnesses would be heard only upon the request of the committee; witnesses would not be allowed counsel; no questions could be asked witnesses except by committee counsel; no written questions could be put to witnesses through committee counsel. Counsel for the Teachers Union protested the prohibition of the right of witnesses to have counsel and to permit the cross-examination of committee witnesses, but to no avail. He also attempted repeatedly to interpolate questions from the floor until upon two occasions he was ejected from the proceedings and another time barred from attendance.[16] The committee was within its legal rights in imposing these limitations upon the procedure. It can be argued that in a hearing where the consequences might have such far-reaching effect upon those involved the committee would have been well advised to lean over backward in ex-

[16] Controversy arose over the incident of ejection. William J. Mulligan, counsel for the Teachers Union, alleged that he had been needlessly roughed up by the guards who carried out the committee chairman's order to remove him; to support his claim he offered evidence that he had required medical attention as a result of injuries incurred. Committee counsel bluntly denied the charge as an unwarranted and wholly unsupported distortion of the true facts. Ten years after the event the possibility of ascertaining the true facts is conjectural because recollected events assume such form that fact and fancy defy separation. The preponderance of evidence—or opinion—strongly suggests that the Teachers Union counsel was handled more severely than the conditions warranted. Press comment at the time, sketches by newspaper artists, and depositions by the person concerned are corroborated by statements of persons present when the incident occurred. It should be added that the persons who have expressed this opinion were not sympathetic to the position taken by the Teachers Union.

The incident is of no great interest, but it is related because it does have some significance as an index of attitudes. Neither the Coudert committee chairman nor its counsel believed in strong arm methods and certainly they had no intention of directing their staff to commit physical abuse; yet they were so convinced of the utter lack of justification of anyone's seeking to challenge their authority that they felt resistance justified the use of force.

At various times in the course of the investigation, the actions of the accused teachers and of the Teachers Union was criticized by the committee as typical of the tactics of the Communist Party. The union was a vigorous unrelenting foe. It fought to win and in so doing eagerly seized upon every opportunity to get in a telling blow without giving much consideration to the amenities. Union officials took the view that while the committee operated through legally recognized channels and observed the letter of the law in procedural matters, the entire investigation violated the spirit of American institutions. Proceeding from this promise, these officials felt justified in employing rather elemental methods to combat the investigation in all its aspects.

tending courtesies and safeguards to those who might suffer injury.

Some aspects of the public hearings also seem to reveal certain attitudes and states of mind on the part of committee members or counsel or both. There was a marked contrast between the interest shown by the committee itself in the hearings where the witnesses were called by the committee to expose alleged Communists and those in which the individuals concerned appeared to present their defense. In the first instance the full membership was in attendance; in the later hearings only one or two members of the committee were ordinarily present, frequently, only one. This situation strongly suggests that the later hearings were rather *pro forma* or at least so regarded by the committee itself. This impression is fortified by the statements of Senator Coudert and the committee counsel from time to time as they attempted to persuade testifying witnesses to limit their statements.

Committee witnesses had been permitted, even encouraged, to go into minute detail in telling their stories. At times some of them seemed to digress somewhat unnecessarily, yet they were never called to account. Almost from the beginning the responding witnesses were adjured to hurry along, to restrict their statements to a consideration of the specific charges made against them. When Charles J. Hendley, president of the Teachers Union, took the witness stand, he attempted to read a statement presenting the union's reasons for resisting the committee's efforts to obtain the list of union members. He was repeatedly interrupted by Mr. Windels, who questioned him extensively on matters relating to the International Workers Order, which according to Mr. Hendley had nothing to do with the Teachers Union. When he was finally permitted to read his statement, Senator Coudert continued to hurry him along until Assemblyman Irwin Steingut, an *ex officio* member of the committee, asserted that he thought Mr. Hendley should have as much time as he wanted. Thereafter he was permitted to finish his statement uninterrupted.

Later, when the individuals named were given their opportunity to make public statements, there were numerous attempts to expedite proceedings. On the second day Senator Coudert announced that in order to make greater headway each witness would be allowed only five minutes to read his general statement.[17] The chairman explained that, inasmuch as the chief objective of the witness was to get his statement into the record, he could submit it to the committee, and if it was relevant, it would be marked in evidence and made immediately available to the press. Actually, the committee was never able to adhere to the five-minute rule; although there was constant fencing back and forth between the witness and the committee counsel over what was and what was not relevant, each witness did succeed in getting considerable material into the record.[18]

The question of relevancy is of particular importance in a proceeding of this kind. The general charge against all of those involved in the hearing was that they were members of the Communist Party. In some instances committee witnesses were able to supply more detail by recounting particular party activities engaged in by the persons under consideration. For example, some persons were described as having participated actively in putting out the *Teacher-Worker;* others were active in the numerous party meetings; still others engaged in teaching and writing for party educational programs. All of these things, in some measure at least, were concrete enough to permit rather specific answers, even though in many instances neither the charge nor the answer was susceptible of absolute

[17] *Public Hearings,* p. 951.

[18] The following day Senator Farrell, acting committee chairman, extended the time to ten minutes, but this limit was little more observed than before (*Ibid.,* p. 1200).

proof because of the clandestine character of most of the activity in question.

In other instances, however—and they were by no means isolated or exceptional—the charge was simply that particular persons were Communists because they had attended closed meetings of the party. No supporting detail was introduced in some instances, and in others the only supplementary information was a recollection of a particular incident, discussion, or conversation allegedly participated in by the individual named. Yet in the face of such a general charge, unsupported except by the testimony of witnesses whose inaccuracy in particular instances had been demonstrated, the accused individual was faced with the task of clearing his name in the only official hearing which stood between him and suspension from his job.

In this situation the question of relevance of testimony was delicate. In the absence of specific charges which could be answered specifically, the individuals named as Communists were obliged to fall back upon answers of a more general order. Character references, testimonials of teaching ability, declarations that they had not used their classes for Communist indoctrination, evidence of scholarly activity and professional growth, and other similar material constituted the bulk of the testimony offered in rebuttal.

Toward material of this character Senator Coudert and his staff took a rather skeptical attitude. Numerous instances crop up where witnesses who sought to introduce such matter were interrupted and hampered by the committee. Repeatedly the witness was cautioned to confine his statement to comment upon the charges made against him. It is not clear what the committee had in mind because in those instances where the only charge was party membership, the only defense was evidence that the person accused had not engaged in activities which Communists were said to do. Nonindoctrination in classroom, great exertion in scholarship, and general excellence in work all seemed to have considerable relevance under these conditions.[19]

The following colloquy is representative of the attitude taken by the committee:

Senator Coudert: The committee will be happy to hear anything bearing upon the limited question of whether or not Mr. Canning or any other witness told the truth with respect to your participation in Communist activities of the City College Unit and bearing upon your professional and character background. I think that is quite sufficient as a foundation for the committee or any other interested body to form conclusions as to who is telling the truth. . . . You are here solely by the courtesy of this committee, which has no obligation whatsoever to permit you to be heard, to give you an opportunity now on the public record to deny the assertions to which you take exception. You have denied those assertions categorically. The record is quite clear on that. You have closed the record; there is nothing left unsaid. If you wish to say a few words in further explanation, you may do so in a very limited fashion.[20]

While in the statement just quoted, Mr. Coudert did acknowledge that character references and professional qualifications were relevant, he did not always reflect this view in his treatment of particular witnesses. On one occasion the following exchange took place:

Witness: . . . In fact, since this charge was made public, I have received many unsolicited letters from former and present students which prove that I never engaged in such an activity. Some of these will now be read into the record.
Senator Coudert: No they will not be read into the record.
Witness: Senator Coud——
Senator Coudert: I am not going to argue the matter.

[19] These charges are discussed below, p. 169.
[20] *Public Hearings,* p. 1042.

Witness: Mr. Canning specifically stated in my case Communist propaganda was introduced into the classroom.

Senator Coudert: You will please observe the instruction of the Committee. You are making a statement and we are quite prepared to accept the statement, your statement of the proof. You say you have letters to buttress it. Those letters will be filed and placed in evidence and made available to anyone who wants to consider them. The Committee cannot go on for an indefinite time. . . .

Witness: I think I have adhered myself to the testimony.

Senator Coudert: I am not debating that.

Witness: I feel that since Mr. Canning stated at great length that I have indoctrinated my students with Communist propaganda, I should be permitted to read at least a few letters.

Senator Coudert: They go into the record and we have your statement that there is a substantial number of letters.[21]

Actually the witness did succeed in reading one letter into the record—a very impressive testimonial from Captain William Dooley, Quartermaster Corps, U.S. Army, who had been a member of the New York City police department at the time he had taken work at City College. Stating that his letter was unsolicited, he said in part:

The Instructor made no attempt to veer from the subject matter of the course, and if any student offered a distorted interpretation of the material being discussed in class, Mr. —— made a special effort to correct this view held by the student. . . . I was also impressed by the fact that Mr. —— never attempted to stifle the expression of opinion on the part of the students, always cautioning, however, that students should base their judgments upon careful reading rather than upon mere opinion.[22]

By persistent effort the witness subsequently succeeded in getting several letters into evidence by title and author, al-

[21] *Ibid.,* pp. 1154–1156.   [22] *Ibid.,* pp. 1157–1159.

though not by text. His portion of the hearing is sprinkled by such statements from Senator Coudert as the following:

If you have any additional letters of that character they can be marked into evidence. . . .
Will you file those letters. We might have a thousand letters and a thousand exhibits. . . .
How much more time are you going to take?
I must ask you to respect my ruling. You are only wasting your time and my time. You can file those and state from whom they are.[23]

From the foregoing, several points should be noted. The committee looked upon the public hearings very differently than did the accused individuals. The evidence which it had received from its own witnesses had already convinced the committee of the guilt (of party membership) of the teachers named. The public hearings were not considered by the committee as an opportunity for learning more facts about subversive activities, hence the attitude of relative indifference to the substantive character of what each witness had to present. The committee members were more concerned with expediting the proceedings than with examining the witnesses. In fact, except for being asked explicitly whether they were or were not Communists, most of those who appeared were permitted to make their statement and withdraw without a single word of cross-examination by the committee or counsel.

It may be observed in passing that the public hearing did have a significant legal aspect. No person was suspended from his post until he had publicly stated under oath that he was not a member of the Communist Party. Several charges were made against each person suspended, but in every case the essential legal ground upon which suspension and, later, re-

23 *Ibid.*, pp. 1159–1162.

moval was based was "conduct unbecoming a teacher," one of the grounds for removal enumerated in the teachers' tenure law. When a teacher was publicly named by a committee witness as a member of the Communist Party, he was summoned before the legislative committee in public session and compelled to declare under oath whether he was a Communist. When he denied that he was a party member he was suspended from his teaching position and the conduct committee of the Board of Higher Education brought perjury charges against him. The fact that each person named was notified by subpoena to appear, that the only point stressed by the committee was the direct question of party membership, and that disciplinary action by school authorities followed almost immediately upon this ceremony suggests that the sequence was not accidental.

In spite of repeated statements that proceedings had to move along and that witnesses should limit themselves to matters strictly relevant, most of those testifying succeeded, if they were persistent, in getting considerable material into the record. The chairman or counsel, after initial resistance, would usually end by permitting the witness to go ahead. This acquiescence, grudging though it was, undoubtedly reflected a genuine desire on the part of the committee to be fair and considerate. The difficulty lay in the completely different conceptions of the hearings entertained by the two parties.

The same interpretation may be applied to the treatment of letters of testimony and similar supporting data. The committee felt that the interests of those accused would be adequately protected if such matter were accepted as part of the public record. To the person who wished to establish his innocence of party membership, and also to the one who wanted to prove that he had not used his classroom as a vehicle for proselytizing his students, the privilege of having his rebuttal go into the record had little appeal.

There was no guarantee that such material would ever see the light of day unless by reading it himself he could get it into the verbatim transcript of the hearing. The lack of faith in the efficacy of having letters accepted for the record was justified both by contemporary and subsequent events. There is no indication that the press reported anything except the testimony actually given at the public hearings. On this score, the accused was deprived of a fair hearing so far as the general public was concerned. In the case of the committee witnesses the public got the entire story; in the case of those who attempted to present their side, the public's view was restricted.

Even the members of the committee were shortchanged. Earlier reference has been made to the poor committee attendance at the public hearings during the time when responding witnesses had their day. The presence of a single committee member contrasted sharply with the full attendance during the appearance of the committee's own accusing witnesses and provided further evidence of the committee's attitude toward the hearing.

Where attendance was so poor there seemed to be all the more reason why the verbatim record should be as full as possible, unless it could be assumed that absentee members would give careful scrutiny to all exhibits. This assumption seems unwarranted in view of subsequent disclosures. Persons close to the investigation have recently stated that with the exception of the chairman, members of the committee never examined any of the exhibits or read the final report submitted by the committee.

The failure of the committee and the respondents to reach an accord on the public hearings lay in their different concepts concerning the purpose which the hearings were to serve. The committee looked upon the hearings solely as a gesture of generosity on its own part—a courtesy extended, not an obligation met. Since the committee acknowledged no obligation, any action according the accused a public hearing was voluntary and gratuitous, and it ill befitted the beneficiaries to complain over the treatment they received.

To the persons publicly charged to be Communists, the public hearing held an entirely different significance. Their names had been spread upon the public record. Although as yet no official charges had been filed against them, statements issued by the school authorities had left no doubt that unless those named could clear themselves, their professional careers were in jeopardy. The first and possibly the only public proceeding in which they might have an opportunity to rebut and refute the allegations that they were Communists was the public hearing of the Coudert committee. It is not surprising under these circumstances that the accused teachers looked upon these hearings as crucial and left no possibility unexploited in their efforts to present the fullest evidence possible. What to the committee was a formality, was to the accused a possible turning point in their lives. That they should appraise the public hearings upon the basis of radically different standards was inevitable.

The foregoing review of policy and procedural decisions which played a vital part in shaping the outcome of the investigation has already thrown considerable light upon the committee's operating assumptions. Attention will now be turned to a more intensive scrutiny of these assumptions in order to ascertain (1) what the committee's objectives were; (2) what premises it proceeded from in pursuing its investigation; (3) whether its public declarations and its practices were identical or, at least, reconcilable.

It is important to understand what the committee interpreted its own task to be. Under the resolution it was instructed by the legislature to ascertain and report "the extent to which, if any, subversive activities may have been permitted to be carried on in the schools and colleges of such educational system."

In the committee's final report it interpreted the legislative directive to mean that "the committee's duty was to establish the extent and pattern of subversive activities in the schools. The exposure of individuals engaged therein was a necessary incident to the ascertainment of the pattern." From its study of Communist literature, the committee was convinced that the purpose of the party was subversive so far as American institutions were concerned. It concluded that anyone who joined the party was engaged in subversive activity. Its own task, therefore, was to find out how many Communists there were among the teachers and students of the city schools and colleges, who they were, and through what organizations they operated. An extract from the committee's interim report confirms this view:

The Communist Party is not a political party as that term has historically been understood in this country. It is a political conspiracy aimed both at the social structure and the political framework of this nation. Since it is a conspiracy, the persons actively engaged in it are conspirators.[24]

The point is elaborated in the final report:

The results of our investigation show that there is no inconsistency between the concept of freedom of political belief and the conclusion that Communists cannot be permitted to hold employment in the public schools. This is because Communist Party membership does not mean merely the acceptance of certain political and social objectives: the Party commits its members to a discipline and a course of conduct which are incompatible with the public service, in that they are thereby obliged to do improper acts in furtherance of those objectives. Thus, in every case uncov-

[24] *Interim Report*, p. 5.

113

ered by the Committee, the very act of joining the Party was tainted with fraud when the neophyte was instructed to assume an alias for party purposes, and to conceal the fact of his membership from all outsiders. The evidence shows this to be standard party procedure, firmly rooted in the basic philosophy of Communism and applicable to all members except Party spokesmen, who must necessarily be publicly known as Communists. Party members are not permitted to select their own ethical standards: whatever the Party orders is right and may not be questioned. Consequently, the very acceptance of Communist Party membership is, in and of itself, an overt act incompatible with the public service.[25]

In his introductory remarks, Committee Counsel Paul Windels declared that the committee was not concerned with people's beliefs: "Our country is not endangered either by freedom of opinion or freedom of speech, even if used to advocate political doctrines or social theories which are abhorrent to the vast majority of our people." [26]

Concerning political activity he explained, "it has always been the American method to respect the right of every man and woman in our democracy to his or her own political beliefs; to organize political parties with a right to a place on the ballot; to advocate change in our social order or form of government, *provided they do so openly and in accordance with the principles of decency and fair play and do not misuse positions of public trust or confidence in so doing.*" [27]

Mr. Windels seems to place the emphasis upon open action. Advocacy of change is not subversive so long as it is carried on in the open. Yet in its first report the committee states:

Even if such party activity [Communist] has been engaged in openly and with the candor generally exercised by adherents of

[25] *Final Report,* p. 10.
[26] *First Report,* Legislative Document (1941), No. 54, p. 61.
[27] *Ibid.,* pp. 60–61. Italics added.

political parties in a democracy, even if such activity had not sought to undermine our democratic form of government, *it is a serious question whether such complete and unremitting absorption with political activity as is indicated would be proper under any circumstances among organized groups of public employees.*[28]

Unless those words mean something other than a straightforward interpretation conveys, the position taken here is that teachers should not engage actively in political matters. To those convinced that the chief objective of the Rapp-Coudert committee was the destruction of the Teachers Union, Mr. Windels' statement of the qualifications which political activity must conform to if it is to remain within the orbit of respectability is not likely to allay suspicion. Such expressions as "principles of decency and fair play" and "complete and unremitting absorption with political activity" hardly convey precise and definable standards for judgment. In an area where civil liberties are involved, such indefinite, hence subjective, canons of conduct afford no guidance or protection to those affected. The terminology has no established meaning. It neither informs the regulated of the permissible limits of acceptable activity nor steadies the hand of the regulator by providing a frame of reference within which he can maintain a faithful course.

At the outset the committee made a special point of stressing its complete indifference to what the teachers thought and said. The exact words of Mr. Windels, committee counsel, have already been quoted. It seems appropriate to compare this view with specific instances where the question of opinions was raised in the committee's investigations.

On December 9, 1940, when Charles J. Hendley, president of the Teachers Union, was on the witness stand, Mr. Windels quoted from statements by Isidore Begun, a former member of

[28] *Ibid.,* p. 65. Italics added.

the union and an avowed Communist, that the Teachers Union accepted the fact of the class struggle and that the capitalist system was a "rotten system," and then asked, "Do you think that a person entertaining those views should be a teacher in the Public Schools?" [29]

It will be remembered that most of the responding witnesses were permitted to make their statements before the committee without cross-examination. In almost every case where cross-examination did occur it dealt chiefly with two points: the witness' participation in the May Day parade of 1938 and the witness' speaking or writing activities. In one representative case, for example, the witness was questioned at length about his writing for the *New Masses* and other proletarian and revolutionary publications. Excerpts from his writings were read back to him and he was asked to comment whether they did not reveal his belief in the class struggle. He was asked to explain why he used the term "comrade" in his writings if he had not accepted the ideological beliefs of Marxism.[30]

Questions of this character seem to reflect great interest in what the witness believed and what he said or wrote. Furthermore, in this instance there was no problem of hidden identity. When the witness had written the articles in question, he had written under his own name, and they had been published in journals which circulated freely. There is, of course, the possibility that Mr. Windels was indifferent to the fact that the individual held these opinions and was merely asking these questions in order to prove that he was a Communist. It is impossible to be sure which point the committee considered more important.

On another occasion a witness was questioned closely about his part in publishing the paper, *Fag-an-Ballach,* termed by the committee an "Irish revolutionary sheet." The paper, which published only an issue or two and then disappeared,

---

[29] *Public Hearings,* pp. 62–65. [30] *Ibid.,* pp. 1231–1245.

was alleged to have been a Communist propaganda instrument. In the course of the questioning, Senator Farrell, the committee member present, was especially attracted by an editorial based upon the poem, "The Deserted Village." He read into the record the sentence, "Oliver Goldsmith's description of the deserted village where wealth accumulated and men decay was as true of Ireland yesterday as it is of the great powerful country in which we live," and asked the witness, "Do you mean to imply by that statement that American democracy is decaying in any way?" [31] The question of opinions persisted in intruding itself.

Communist Activity in the New York City Schools

If one takes the committee on its own terms, its task did not extend to the necessity of proving that membership in the Communist Party in 1940–1941 actually was subversive in the sense that it was a dangerous threat to democratic institutions. To the committee, party membership was *ipso facto* subversive activity. It is of interest, therefore, to see what sort of activity the Communist Party and its teacher members engaged in, in order to grasp more clearly the nature of the threat which they imposed, in the eyes of the committee.

Only fifty pages of its final report of almost four hundred pages is devoted to the specific activities of the Communist groups in the New York City schools; fourteen of these fifty pages merely reproduce extracts from the party publications to illustrate the kind of party propaganda deemed subversive by the committee. Quantitative measurements are not necessarily significant; but one cannot help but speculate over the paucity of information which would demonstrate the dangerous nature of the party's activity. A review of these activities as set forth by the committee report follows.

The Communist Party infiltrated the College Teachers

[31] *Ibid.*, p. 1289.

Union. Figures cited by the committee indicate that the College Teachers Union had a membership of approximately one
thousand and that the number of Communists in the union approximated one hundred. By carefully organizing its
strength and concentrating its voting power upon candidates
agreed upon beforehand, the Communist fraction was able
to capture some of the offices and influence the policies of the
union in spite of its comparatively small proportion of the
total membership. Irregular attendance of most union members and general apathy in matters of program simplified the
job for the well-organized energetic Communists. On those
occasions when union membership was out in strength, party
members resorted to such devices as interminable debate,
points of order, technicalities, and other forms of disruptive tactics until members, wearied by the sterility of the proceedings, left the meeting, whereupon the party would take
over.

Evidence was also introduced by the former Communists
who were chiefly instrumental in supplying the committee
with most of its information that membership in the party
imposed heavy financial burdens. Besides regular monthly
dues, frequent special assessments and other contributions
were exacted. In addition, each member was required to subscribe to certain party publications and to buy large quantities
of miscellaneous party literature.

Communists were required to perform certain duties for the
party. Among these were the sale and distribution of party
literature and the pasting up of party stickers bearing slogans
such as "Defend the Soviet Union," "All Out for May Day,"
"Vote for Browder and Ford," etc.

At the weekly meeting of the party groups the members
engaged in long discussions of party policy, Marxian dialectic,
international politics, and a wide variety of ideological issues

118

which only Communists would find interesting enough to indulge in. They would also subject themselves to what they called self-criticism, during which each person would attempt to analyze his own weaknesses and then invite comment and suggestion from his fellow members in order that he might become a better Communist.

A point stressed in the committee report, again chiefly on the basis of the testimony of the person referred to above, was that the party made such heavy demands on the time of its members that it prevented them from engaging in professional work. The Communist Party was pictured as belittling scholarly research as childish, puerile, politically immature. A member's time could be more profitably spent in furthering the party program, recruiting new members, engaging in union activity, contributing to party publications.

This argument is hardly convincing for a number of reasons. In the first place, it is irrelevant and immaterial in the context presented. If the committee were concerned with the professional qualities of the teaching staff as indicated by scholarly publication, then the dissipation and diversion of energy to organizational activities would certainly become an appropriate subject of inquiry. To term such diversion subversive seems farfetched. Much more persuasive factors in the comparatively small volume of research and writing produced by the faculties of the city colleges have been the heavy teaching loads and the low salaries which have forced faculty members to take on additional work such as evening classes in order to supplement their incomes.

Actually, however, the charge that those alleged to be Communists had been most negligent in keeping up their professional standards was not supported by the facts. At the time of the public hearings, several of those who had been named as active party members presented documentary evidence of extensive research activity during the years they were supposed to be devoting so much time to the party.[32] The committee does not attempt to explain this patent contradiction. The reader cannot help but wonder about the general credibility of testimony which seems to be so vulnerable to challenge on specific points.

The committee made much of the subversive character of the *Teacher-Worker*. This monthly newspaper at the City College and its Brooklyn College counterpart, *The Staff*, were published clandestinely by the Communist units at the two colleges from the spring of 1935 until February, 1939. These papers have been termed vicious, scurrilous, libelous. The question arises: What constitutes subversion in a newspaper? Does its anonymous character automatically make it subversive? If the answer to this question is affirmative, nothing remains to be considered. If a periodical circulated anonymously contained only noncontroversial matters to which no one could take exception, would it still be classified as subversive because of the hidden identity of its author? If the answer in this case is negative, then the question of subversion apparently depends more upon what the paper says than upon its underground character. Let us apply this test to the *Teacher-Worker*.

From a careful and thorough sampling of the various issues of the *Teacher-Worker* throughout the more than four years of its publication, the following observations seem warranted: The tone of the paper was invariably critical, militantly opposed to capitalism, the vested interests, the college administration; in its effort to be the outspoken advocate of the teacher's interests, the paper was sometimes insolent; it frequently exaggerated and was not above twisting the facts in a particular situation for the sake of embellishing a good tale. On the other hand, it did not incite to violence; it did print

[32] *Ibid.*, pp. 1006–1021, 1088–1104, 1137–1139, 1200–1228, 1261–1269, 1312–1330, 1413–1426, 1459–1465, 1491–1516, 1520–1541, 1557–1573.

corrections and retractions when individuals indicated that it had misrepresented them. Finally, the paper stated plainly on its masthead that it was published by the Communist unit on the campus and thus put its readers on notice as to the kind of paper it was. No one was compelled to read it; there was no compulsion to believe its contents. It is difficult to see how, under these circumstances, the paper could be taken seriously enough to be regarded as subversive.

The *Final Report* of the committee includes several representative extracts from the *Teacher-Worker* and *The Staff* to illustrate their subversive character. Two of the most extreme examples are here reproduced with the report's accompanying comments.

Foremost, however, among the "lackeys of Wall Street" was the late President Robinson, the prime object of Communist hatred at the City College.

How dare Robinson slander the Soviet Union, where every student is paid a salary as a "worker in training," and is sure of a position when he is graduated! The Soviet plans for 1936 call for more than 4,000 new schools and a 20 per cent increase of students in pedagogical schools. Why can we not "plan" for obviously necessary expansion here at City College? Is it not because the only planning done here is to increase the flow of profits to the bankers? How else was our City budget planned? And all of Robinson's planning now is how to fit the College budget to the banker's requirements, not to educational ones. Such is free higher education under capitalism.

(*Teacher-Worker,* March 1936, Vol. I, No. 12, p. 4)

Perhaps as revealing as any material printed in *"The Staff"* is the following comment on an article published in Harper's by a teacher who had joined the party and resigned in disgust:

A professor of history in one of our universities faced by the growing challenge of reaction both within the school and without, and having suffered economically as a result of the depression, becomes active in progressive movements and eventually joins the Communist Party. To his dismay he "discovers" that a Communist Party Unit is not a social club but a serious revolutionary organization; that it makes incessant demands upon a member's time and money; that everyone—even a college professor with a touch of the snob about him—is expected to do his share.

—— —— disliked the "conspiratorial" air which surrounds the work of the Communist Party. Courageous soul! But strangely enough when his wife is assigned the task of introducing the *New Masses* into the Faculty Wives Clubrooms, he is again dismayed lest she expose herself as a radical!

Perhaps the secret of the professor's disillusionment is to be sought in his contempt for the bookkeeper. The notion that he could learn anything from a person without an academic degree seems appalling. What indeed could —— —— learn from an ordinary working man? The class struggle, the need for unity, for organization, militancy, courage and honesty, solidarity and *action!*

(*The Staff*, August 1937, Vol. III, No. 12, p. 3.) [33]

The next indictment drawn against the Communist teachers is perhaps the most fundamental of all. The teachers concerned were charged with utilizing their jobs as vantage points to sow seeds of discontent and propagate their doctrine by recruiting party members among their students.

Allegation versus Proof

It is one thing to condemn the practice of using the school to indoctrinate students and recruit Communists. It is another to prove conclusively the existence and extent of such activity in any given situation. This difficulty was present in a large degree in the New York schools inquiry. Lacking party records which would reveal not only members but their sponsors at the time of affiliation, the committee was forced to rely upon other types of information to test its hypothesis.

From a careful examination of the very extensive Communist literature on the subject, the committee was aware of the party emphasis upon the schools as one of the most fruitful media for building its membership. It was logical to assume

[33] *Final Report*, pp. 284–285.

that the energetic organizations already known to be functioning in New York schools were not overlooking the students.
Furthermore, more tangible evidence was available.

Specifically the allegations of teacher-student relationship
were: frequent comment upon student activity in the *Teacher-
Worker* and *The Staff;* continuous appearances of known
Communist members of the college faculties as speakers at the
meetings of such Communist front organizations as the American Student Union and the various Marxist study groups.
These speakers invariably discussed subjects then being emphasized by the *Daily Worker* and faithfully expounded the
party line then current. As the line changed so did the speakers. Known Communists functioned as faculty advisers to the
Marxist study groups. All of this information was obtainable
from public records. The committee was not successful in
turning up more concrete information through its interviews.

The charge that Communist teachers used their classrooms
for indoctrinating students was made by the committee. On
this charge, which seems most serious of all and certainly raises
questions of continued fitness as teachers, the evidence is
largely derived and hearsay in character. The committee's
chief witness testified that classroom indoctrination was continuously stressed and that frequent discussions were devoted
to the problem of effective classroom techniques. He indicated
that certain members of the group had attained great *expertise*
in presenting basic party concepts through their course lec-
tures. He gave examples of how this could be done, but he
could not testify that he had actually seen it done because he
had not attended the classes himself.

None of the witnesses presented by the committee at its
public hearings testified to specific examples of classroom indoctrination. On the other hand, many of the teachers named
as Communists were able to present extensive testimonials
from students and former students declaring that no effort had

been made to present slanted opinions in the classes they had attended. At least some of these testimonials came from individuals who could not in any way be suspected of entertaining sympathy for communism. The possibility always exists that the presentation had been so subtle that its victims were completely unaware. Such subtlety, if possible, would be of questionable effectiveness.

From the viewpoint of the committee, its case against the offending teachers was not weakened by the absence of concrete corroborative evidence. The presence of Communists as college instructors and the knowledge of party strategy along with the assertions of persons formerly belonging to the party added up to present a case which convinced the committee. To the outsider the arguments are not so convincing. Conceding the presence of known Communists on the faculty and acknowledging the probability that they would desire to win disciples among the students, including those in their own classes, it seems strange that the committee was unable to produce evidence more tangible and more substantial than it did. Surely its explanation that it did not wish to injure young people by exposing them to public censure would not apply to students who had never had contact with the Communist Party or its front organizations. Nor was there serious danger that students who supplied corroborative evidence might suffer injury through retaliation. No one connected with the inquiry was ever threatened with or suffered bodily harm. Furthermore, it would not have been necessary to divulge names of individuals who supplied specific evidence of classroom indoctrination. The committee could have reproduced the important testimony without disclosing the witness. This procedure was followed in reproducing other information. That no such testimony is presented in the reports treating this subject must be interpreted to indicate that none existed.

There is no desire to labor the point, but it seems that the issue of classroom indoctrination is one of the most important of the entire inquiry. The presence of subversive activities in the schools is the question the committee has been directed to ascertain. To a considerable degree the committee proceeds from the assumption that subversive activity and Communist activity is identical, hence proof of the presence of some Communists in the schools constitutes proof that subversive activity exists. The committee reasons that if teachers are Communists, they must indoctrinate students, therefore are guilty of subversive activity. The absence of substantial corroborative evidence is immaterial. But a position equally tenable, *in the absence of corroborative evidence,* is: if the known Communist teachers are employing their classrooms to indoctrinate students with communism and are doing so by deliberate, conscious trickery and fraud, they are guilty of subversive activity. The test in this case would be concrete evidence; without it innocence would have to be assumed.

This is not a matter of splitting dialectical hairs. It is based upon the premise that membership in the Communist Party is not *ipso facto* subversive activity and upon further premise that culpability in the case of alleged subversive activity should be objectively established by evidence about what the person did. If this test is applied in the case of the New York teachers, it is submitted that the committee did not prove its case.

No one can read through the verbatim testimony, even with the abridgements already discussed, without being impressed with the generally superior character of the group here under scrutiny. There seems no doubt from evidence presented elsewhere that some of the group were Communists, but the impressive and inescapable fact is that the *only evidence presented by either side* points to: (1) outstanding scholarship, (2) superior teaching; (3) absence of indoctrination in the classroom.

Each of the persons called before the committee testified

under oath that he was not a Communist. Some of them lied; it seems overwhelmingly certain that others did not. To the committee this one falsehood, plus the fact of membership, was proof that the *individual* was engaged in subversive activity, hence unfit to remain a teacher. To this writer the factual record does not support this conclusion. Surely if these people were as dangerous as alleged, there should be more discernible evidence of their misdeeds.

In the case of several persons whose membership in the Communist Party seems to be established beyond doubt, their records of training, achievement, and advancement are so impressive that they should raise serious doubts as to the relevancy of party membership.[34] If party membership made the heavy time demands that the committee's informers alleged, and if these people were yet able to compile records of achievement such as those presented, either these people could not be practicing Communists or they were so outstanding that the mere fact of their party membership was of minor importance.

This point is particularly troublesome because there is so little to indicate that the committee was sufficiently diligent in searching for evidence that each person named as a Communist had in fact permitted his membership to affect his work. Most of the alleged Communists were instructors, hence vulnerable to the general charge of indoctrinating students through classroom work. If this general indictment had substance, it should not have been too difficult to marshal concrete evidence against particular individuals. Not only is such evidence lacking, but one searches in vain for any indication that the committee made a serious attempt to obtain it. There is nothing in the public hearings, either in the testimony of the committee witnesses or in the cross-examination of the re-

[34] Recently much emphasis has been laid on the argument that the real factor which disqualifies Communists as teachers is that they are no longer free to seek and teach the truth. This point is discussed below. See p. 217.

spondents, to suggest that this point was emphasized. The committee reports do not indicate that the committee tried to investigate this point but failed.

Was there an a priori assumption that Communist membership was synonymous with classroom indoctrination and other conduct deemed reprehensible? The evidence available points to this conclusion. It is fortified by the treatment accorded the nonteaching members of the college staffs. There was no possibility that they could abuse their trust and indoctrinate unsuspecting students if this was the real danger from Communists, and, without exception, their employment records indicated outstanding achievement; yet they were in effect condemned by formula: They were Communists, therefore, they were subversive.

The deductive reasoning which dominated the investigating committee and later the Board of Higher Education was costly in its toll on high-grade personnel; furthermore, it seems likely that psychologically the effect was unfortunate. Some of the group named as Communists and subsequently separated from the city colleges were individuals of great personal charm, intellectual distinction, demonstrated capacity for leadership, high initiative, and courage. Even though their number was few, they were an important segment of the colleges' intellectual resources. This much is a statement of fact; the record is there to prove it.

But there is food for thought in the entire incident, and it bears generally upon the broad question of academic freedom and communism. Some of these able people were Communists, but they had joined the party by choice and not because of coercion. True enough, they joined in publishing a paper that sometimes far overstepped the boundaries of urbane good taste by pointing fingers and calling names, and that understandably gave serious offense. Further, they sought to control certain non-Communist organizations and thus engaged in activity which affected other people. This is not a very impressive bill of particulars, but the fact that these individuals saw fit to operate anonymously rather than out in the open seems to have added considerably to the magnitude of their sin.

Inasmuch as they had joined of free will, and defections had occurred periodically without bodily injury being done to the deserters, does it not seem possible, even likely, that many of these individuals might have left the party voluntarily as the facts about communism and Communist methods became more understood? A question that may well be asked is whether the American struggle against communism might not have been better served by a group of able, respected ex-Communists in the city colleges to neutralize the effect of those who remained? In short, might not the case for democratic institutions be psychologically much stronger than it is where communism can be combated only by liquidating Communists? These questions may not yield a single answer to which all will assent. They deserve, however, to be asked and considered before decisive action is taken to purge the instructional staffs of those who may at any given moment be under suspicion.

The Teachers' Unions and the Communist Party

The relationship between the teachers' unions, the Communist Party, and the activities of the Coudert committee call for special attention. At no time during the investigation was adequate attention given to the importance of clarifying this relationship, nor does the final committee report do much to remove the confusion generated during the investigation. The situation was admittedly complex, but the committee did little to enlighten the public. The clash between the Teachers Union (also the College Teachers Union) and the Coudert committee quickly became the focal point of the investigation.

The union seized the initiative when the resolution creating the committee was approved, and long before the committee was organized a sharp attack was launched against Assemblyman Rapp and Senator Coudert.

The union showed great energy and resourcefulness in pushing its campaign. Press releases, pamphlets, brochures, placards, and throwaways were turned out in volume. All the familiar techniques of the skilled pamphleteer—twisting of issues, distortion of facts, quoting out of context, subtle *non sequiturs*—were brought into play. There was nothing unusual in this action, however. For some years, through its very active legislative representative, the union had taken aggressive positions on all proposals affecting the schools. Although its opposition to the newly created committee was vigorously pressed, the union does not seem to have been any more extreme than usual.

The committee's early decision to concentrate upon the union and the resulting move to subpoena the membership lists must in retrospect be regarded as a most crucial policy decision because of the effect it had upon the alignment of forces on one side or the other. The considerations leading to this decision are thus of interest.

By the time the committee staff had completed its exploratory inquiries, it had reached two assumptions which became its operating premises: (1) the extent of subversive activity in the schools could best be determined by ferreting out and identifying Communists in the faculty and student body; (2) any Communists on the teaching staffs of the city institutions would unquestionably belong to the teachers' unions. The second premise was derived from information that Communist strategy required its teacher members to join and work through employee organizations, specifically the American Federation of Teachers.

The committee was especially influenced during its forma-tive stages by an article entitled "The Schools and the People's Front" which had appeared in *The Communist,* the monthly magazine published by the Communist Party of the U.S.A. The pertinent excerpt of the article in question stated:

The task of the Communist Party must be first and foremost to arouse the teachers to class-consciousness and to organize them into the American Federation of Teachers, which is in the main current of the American Labor movement.[35]

The committee did not assume that all members of the teachers' unions were Communists, but it did believe that every Communist teacher would belong to the union. It concluded that once all union members were isolated, the task of identifying Communists among the faculties would be simplified. The decision to subpoena union membership lists was regarded as a logical means to this end.

From the standpoint of strategy, the decision to concentrate on the teachers' unions was unfortunate; if the committee's logic was sound, its arithmetic and psychology were faulty. No one has ever claimed that more than a relatively small percentage of the seven thousand members of the New York City teachers' unions were Communist Party members. To investigate all of these persons in order to detect a few score or even a hundred party members seems a questionable procedure. Besides being an inefficient, clumsy mode of operation, it inevitably aroused resentment among all union members and stimulated among nonunion people suspicion as to the committee's motives. The events which followed this decision reflected this reaction.

From conversations with former members of the teachers' unions, several conclusions seem warranted. A significant proportion of the officers of all the teachers' unions and of their

[35] Richard Frank, "The Schools and the People's Front," *The Communist,* 15 (May, 1937), 439.

various branches were clearly not Communists. Some of the most bitter resentment against the methods employed by the Coudert committee came from union members who have never been linked with the Communist Party. From among this group came several of the most active adversaries of the committee. They had initially joined the union because of their belief that only through concerted action could teachers obtain much needed reforms in matters pertaining to their professional welfare. Experience had demonstrated the practical value of organized effort. Through the union such tangible results as better salaries, fuller retirement provisions, and greater job security had been achieved.

Charles J. Hendley, president of the Teachers Union, resisted the committee's efforts to obtain the union's membership lists. He did so because of his sincere belief, well fortified by intimate knowledge of trade union history, that by yielding the lists, he might jeopardize his union and its members. Mr. Hendley's devotion to the Teachers Union over the years, dating back well before the Communist issue was ever raised, affords ample proof of his good faith as a bona fide exponent of unionism.

Throughout the life of the inquiry, Mr. Hendley continued to oppose it because he felt that it was a threat to the existence of the union; while he knew that there were Communists in the union, to him that point was irrelevant. So long as they were good union members, he cared nothing about their politics. Mr. Hendley was not the only union member who held this view; there were in fact a great many. He is used here as an example because his part in the inquiry was so prominent.

Union members were not particularly concerned over the question of communism. If a fellow union member was a good worker, willing to give fully of himself in furthering the union's objectives, his co-operation was welcomed. No one spent much time speculating about his party affiliations. This point cannot be too strongly emphasized because while it is deeply important, it is usually overlooked or inadequately weighted. Conversations with a wide range of persons who had participated actively in the work of the unions clearly establish the fact that from the inside the question of communism within the unions was simply not the issue that many outsiders assumed. It was wholly subordinate to the real objective: protection of gains already won and further advancement of the teachers' interests.

Nor can one accept the oft-expressed view that the non-Communists in the union were either fellow travelers or innocent dupes of their shrewder Communist colleagues. Personal acquaintance with some and extended conversations with a number of other persons concerned establish beyond conjecture the high caliber, political sophistication, and intellectual integrity of many of this group.

In the face of these circumstances, to regard union resentment and resistance as a mere Communist tactic is to oversimplify and mislead. By its steadfast adherence to this position, the Coudert committee confused rather than clarified the issue. The possible constructive contribution of the investigation was correspondingly impaired. Communist Party tactics called for vigorous opposition to the investigation. On this point there can be no doubt. Not all who opposed the investigation, however, were Communists. That the Coudert committee failed to keep this vital distinction in mind is made clear by its actions at the time and also by its final report. For example:

It is commonly accepted, and adequately proved, that the Teachers Union is controlled by Communists. If it is controlled by Communists, then the persons who control it, i.e., Mr. Hendley and his associates—are either Communists or the utensils of Communism.[36]

36 *Final Report*, pp. 354–355. See also pp. 215–241.

The committee's failure to be more accurate in its reasoning reduces the validity of its conclusions and recommendations since it tended to interpret all union activity as cynically inspired and lacking in good faith simply because a few Communists who were also union members used the union for their own purposes.

The hypocritical tactics of the Communist members of the union should not pass unnoticed, however. Although they worked and spoke as members of the Teachers Union, they sometimes used it as a screen for furthering objectives of the Communist Party. In other instances their loyalty to union ends was genuine—but only where party and union objectives coincided. The Communist members of the Teachers Union worked with non-Communist union members, but it cannot be said that they co-operated with them.

Statements were made and actions taken in the name of the union that neither the president nor the vast majority knew about or would have approved had they been consulted. Mr. Hendley with a full-time teaching position could devote only limited attention to the inquiry. Necessarily, many decisions had to be made in his absence, but the tendency to take undue advantage of this opportunity became more and more aggravated as time passed.

The same kind of difficulty manifested itself in the relationship between the Communist members of the union and its legal counsel. Early in the inquiry, long before any individuals had been named as Communists, the Teachers Union engaged Mr. William Mulligan, Jr., as counsel. Mr. Mulligan, a Republican, had been a member of the legal staff of Samuel Seabury during the New York State Legislative investigation of New York City government in the early thirties. He was known to be an expert in the law of legislative investigations. No less important was his reputation for being friendly to labor.

Throughout the inquiry Mr. Mulligan gave unstintingly of

his time and energy to represent his clients, the members of the union. Yet throughout his entire service he never received full co-operation from those he was attempting to represent. As a regular procedure he was excluded from the daily strategy sessions held by the union members involved. Only part of the information necessary in their defense was made available to him, and his advice was always caucused upon before individual members acted. Although he tried to insist that no written statement should go out from the union until he had had an opportunity to check it for legal soundness, he frequently found that his request was being evaded.

These details are included not to discredit the union but to show the difficulty of working with it either by the opposition or its own allies. The individual members have already been described as able, personable, attractive. Yet in their relationships growing out of this investigation, they were anything but co-operative. This fact has great relevance in attempting to appraise the procedures of the Coudert committee.

The following excerpt from the *Daily Worker* is part of an editorial written in criticism of a former member of the Communist Party who had given testimony at a public trial. It illustrates graphically the pattern encountered by the committee.

It is the duty of Communists to throw every possible obstacle in the way of conviction of their fellow party members in the courts, to defend these members by all possible means, and absolutely to refuse to give testimony for the state in any form. Testimony of Communists can only be given for the defense of Communists, not for the state and then it must be based on uncompromising defense of the Party and its program and anyone who trades his testimony to the State for personal immunity from prosecution should be unhesitatingly kicked out of the movement.[37]

[37] *Public Hearings*, p. 12.

It was not the Teachers Union, but the things were done in the name of the union; consequently, it had to bear the brunt. Lack of discrimination can be charged to the Communists and to the committee. By utilizing the union and its officials as a front for Communist ends, the party members invited the committee to identify them as synonymous. When the committee ultimately concluded that the union was subversive, it was making a judgment which in the opinion of the writer was too sweeping, but it had been given some ground for so deciding. What should be stressed is that the committee was not unfriendly to union activity, as such, although this charge was repeatedly made against it; it was opposed to this union because it was convinced that it was merely being used as a shield for Communist purposes.

From its reading of Communist literature, the committee was familiar with the use of nonparty organizations as convenient fronts from which to agitate and further party programs. From its co-operating witnesses, the committee was able to corroborate the general pattern, but there were significant gaps in its information; its case was *prima facie* rather than complete. Had the persons under investigation co-operated, the committee could have refined its generalized impressions and arrived at a more accurate approximation of the true facts. Denied this co-operation the committee was faced with the choice of long, laborious investigation to verify the information already in its possession or of breaking the case with what it had. Its decision in favor of the latter course was unfortunate, but understandable.

The committee has been criticized for its failure to employ the public hearing period more effectively as an instrument for turning up more information. Possibly the committee was on sounder ground in the way it proceeded than it has been given credit for. Previous experience with the same witnesses during the private hearing stage had undoubtedly convinced

135

the investigators that nothing productive could be expected from those who were to attend the public hearings. This may also account for the poor committee attendance at the public hearings and for the minimal amount of cross-examination which testifying witnesses received. If this was the explanation of the committee's demeanor, it would have been well-advised to have stated the reason publicly. Once more, failure to gauge adequately the importance of its public relations redounded to the committee's disadvantage.

The Committee's Procedures Appraised

The Coudert committee has been criticized on a number of scores. Its operating premise is open to challenge. It committed itself mentally before all the evidence was in. It employed procedures that were unnecessarily harsh. It did not go far enough in its corroboration of charges before making them public. It reached conclusions that were too sweeping. It underestimated the injustice to innocent individuals that might accrue from its actions no matter how sincere and well-intentioned.

Contrary to the charges of the opposition, however, those carrying on the inquiry proceeded with a great sense of responsibility and an honest desire to protect the innocent. It has already been said that the committee did not go far enough in verifying information before permitting it to be made public. Instances have been cited where injury was occasioned because the committee permitted individuals to be named as Communists when the evidence to support this claim was not beyond challenge. One must not overlook the committee's total record on this point, however. Many persons were named during private sessions of the committee; yet they were never made public or referred to the Boards of Education and Higher Education. Actually great restraint was shown in this matter, a point worthy of emphasis in any attempt to evaluate its work.

The committee took the view that only by naming those persons known to be members of the Communist Party could it perform its task of determining the extent of subversive activities in the school system. While it strove for accuracy in its desire to present a reliable picture of actual conditions, it did not believe that absolute proof in each individual case was necessary. From its various inquiries it had become convinced that Canning's testimony was substantially correct. He presented a list of names, some of which could be corroborated and some of which could not. He insisted he was sure of the names on his list. The committee decided to accept his list, reasoning that since it was not preferring charges, there was no point in being unduly technical. In retrospect, it can be argued that the committee position was sound because several of those named were able to demonstrate their innocence and retain their jobs. But an equally tenable position—and, to the writer at least, a more persuasive one—is the very fact they have been proven innocent emphasizes the harm done them by unnecessarily blackening their names. What the evidence does not show, however, is that there was deliberate intent on the part of the committee or its staff to denigrate either the Teachers Union or its individual members. When the committee had been blocked in its efforts to obtain full detailed information, it had reached the decision to make public such information as it had been able to develop. Whether its decision was the wisest one possible under the circumstances is at best a very difficult question.

The charge voiced by the Teachers Union that the committee deliberately tried to keep the public hearings from being fruitful must be appraised in the context in which it occurred. The futility it had experienced during the private hearings cannot be ignored. On the other hand, it seems likely that the committee would have been the gainer had it attempted to make more of the public hearings. Careful, systematic cross-examination of witnesses might have elicited useful information. Failing in this, the burden of proof would have rested on those who failed to co-operate. As it was, the committee left itself vulnerable to those who wished to create the impression that its intentions were not above question.

Certain other criticisms of the public hearings were not well taken, however. It was alleged that they were held in quarters so limited that the public was excluded and that what space was available was pre-empted by the committee staff or by Coudert people. The public hearings were held in a room which seated two hundred and fifty persons. The committee and its staff totaled only a dozen persons. Remaining space was available for those who got there first. Seats were much in demand because the hearings attracted wide public attention and there was always a waiting line in the hall, but the same condition prevails at every public hearing or trial where public interest is equally intense.

Another point greatly stressed by the Teachers Union's publicity was the private hearing procedure. Charges of star-chamber procedure, grilling of witnesses, and third-degree tactics were hurled at the committee. In a pamphlet entitled *Senator Coudert's Star Chamber; A Report on the Rapp-Coudert: Private Hearings,* dated January, 1941, this phase of the investigation was described.

The pamphlet, which purports to give an accurate picture of the way private hearings were conducted, is filled with such phrases as: "Senator Coudert's inquisition Chambers," "attempts to intimidate students," "harsh and hostile methods of committee counsel," "witnesses are bullied and threatened."

Attention has already been called to certain aspects of the private hearing procedure which seem unjustified and unnecessary. As for the manner in which the private hearings were conducted, however, there is no evidence that witnesses were subjected to coercive procedures. On the contrary, information from widely differing sources indicates that quite the opposite atmosphere prevailed during these sessions. Individuals interviewed have had no adverse criticism in describing the treatment accorded them. In the few instances when this subject was referred to during the public hearings, the impression of friendly and courteous conduct by the questioners during the private hearings was conveyed.

Two instances occurred during the public hearings when witnesses alleged that irregularities had taken place in the private hearings. In each instance, the committee counsel produced the transcript of the private hearing and read the pertinent testimony to the complaining witness; in each case the witness retracted his statement.[38] All of the evidence points to the greatest care on the part of the committee counsel to be scrupulously accurate and fair in its treatment of the responding witnesses.

One of the most striking contrasts between the Coudert committee and its two predecessors was the manner of handling press relations. On a subject so susceptible of blazing headlines and sensational disclosures as Communists in the public schools, the chairman and his staff exhibited a restraint that was quite exemplary. At the opening of the public hearings, Committee Counsel Windels outlined the self-imposed limitations under which the committee intended to operate. Among them he listed, "to refrain from entering into public controversy with persons under inquiry, regardless of provocation, to refrain from making charges in the public press; in short, to adhere strictly to the ascertainment of facts and their orderly presentation." This self-restraining ordinance was observed, with a single exception, notwithstanding the heated

[38] *Ibid.,* pp. 256, 1001.

campaign of extravagant abuse to which the committee and its staff was subjected.

Two incidents shed further light upon the question of publicity. When the committee decided to force the issue of obtaining the membership lists of the Teachers Union and carried its fight into the courts, the point most emphasized by those who opposed this action was that the lists would be made public once they were in the possession of the committee. The committee was careful to maintain the confidential character of the lists, however; even the president of the union has admitted that membership was never disclosed.

The other incident involved a speech by Senator Coudert in which he was quoted as advocating "brutal treatment" for teachers identified as Communists. In a public letter, John Haynes Holmes, chairman of the board of directors of the American Civil Liberties Union, chided Mr. Coudert for his statement, saying that his speech suggested concentration camps and the Gestapo rather than the democratic way. When the Senator wrote Dr. Holmes and explained what he had really said, the latter replied, "I am particularly sorry that my letter was prompted by newspaper reports misleading and thus inaccurate in character. Having suffered from that sort of thing myself, I know full well how you feel." [39]

The criticism might be voiced that the committee only rarely attempted to explain its work through the press. The public hearings were of course reported and the incident of Mr. Windels and the warrant of arrest for Charles J. Hendley have already been mentioned. On one or two other occasions, Senator Coudert either issued press statements or made public addresses in which the work of the inquiry was mentioned.

[39] The report of Senator Coudert's speech and Dr. Holmes's letter are to be found in the *New York Times* of June 4, 1941. Mr. Coudert's letter to Dr. Holmes and Dr. Holmes's reply are in the files of the American Civil Liberties Union.

This does not constitute a very extensive public relations program for an investigation which extended over the greater part of a year. During the same period the Teachers Union, working chiefly through its Committee to Defend Free Public Education, and the independent Committee for Democracy and Intellectual Freedom were extremely articulate in their campaign of disparagement.

For the interested but bewildered outsider who disliked forming a judgment until the facts were all in, the situation was most unsatisfactory. There was at least a grain of truth in each of the arguments advanced by the union, but it required only a little common sense to recognize that the facts were not quite so pat as they seemed. The very immoderation of some of the union's claims was more than enough to raise a doubt in the mind of the careful reader. Yet the Coudert committee did not do a systematic job of meeting each troublesome point squarely and either demolishing it by showing its inaccuracy or at least giving a clear explanation and defense of the committee's position. This would have enabled many fair-minded persons to determine where they stood, and in the vast majority of cases it would have strengthened the position of the committee itself. Although the enemies of the committee have insisted that it had a high-powered press relations section, there is no evidence that such was the case. Rather, it appears that the committee was insufficiently impressed with the importance of keeping the public properly informed; in fact, the point may be made that had the committee given adequate attention to the importance of winning a healthy public approval, it would have handled many of its most touchy problems differently.

Some observers fear that any effort by a legislative committee toward "winning a healthy public approval" or "keeping the public informed" cannot be attempted without irresponsible sensationalism. If this view is sound, the only choice lies between the two extremes of sphinxlike silence and irresponsible sensationalism. I cannot believe that some more acceptable middle ground is beyond human wit and reason. To admit that the forces tending to discourage measured judgments and tempered pronouncements are formidable in an investigation of this nature is not to concede that they defy resolution. Public relations of any governmental undertaking tend to become more troublesome as the subject matter is more immersed in controversy. Investigation of subversive activities achieves almost the ultimate in this respect. For this reason, the agency conducting the investigation is confronted simultaneously with a temptation to play for lurid effects and an opportunity to educate constructively. To avoid sensationalism by striking the opposite extreme of complete silence is not to accept responsibility but to evade it.

Investigations cannot and should not be conducted behind locked doors or drawn curtains lest they absorb unnecessarily the characteristics peculiar to those carried out behind the iron curtain. So long as subversive activity investigations remain a part of American governmental processes, they should be carried on within the public view. If we are offended by the demagoguery or sensationalism of some legislative investigators, it is well to think how much more harmful their viciousness might be if they were under no compulsion to reveal any of their evil handiwork. In the case of even the meanest and least admirable investigation, safeguards of full disclosure just about counterbalance dangers which should not be ignored or minimized.

Happily, however, it does not inevitably follow that such investigations are conducted by the least able or worthy legislator, and to say that the public relations phase of an investigation has frequently been abused is not to acknowledge that it must always be. The argument that because press relations have dangerous potentialities they should be eschewed is reminiscent of the contention that any governmental intervention into the economic system which affects the inexorable functioning of the free market is doomed to failure and should therefore be avoided. Troublesome issues confronting democratic government will not be solved by ignoring their presence.

The Committee Report

At several points references have already been made to various parts of the Coudert committee's final report. Before taking leave of the committee, however, certain other aspects of the report merit consideration. Coming at the end of the inquiry, after the committee had had full opportunity, if it so desired, to review and reconsider assumptions made, actions taken, judgments expressed, the final report should provide the most reliable expression of its considered position on the many controversial issues presented. During the heat of an investigation when the pressure of events compels quick decision and action cannot await full opportunity to deliberate at length, a committee may make hasty choices that it would have avoided under lesser tension. If in retrospect the committee felt that it had employed procedures unnecessarily harsh, or that its function had shifted from that of investigator to prosecutor, or that it had permitted bias, whether initially held or acquired in the course of the investigation, to spoil its objectivity, the final report would afford an opportunity to harmonize its true feelings with any earlier aberrations which might have occurred.

Several portions of the report do deal with some of the most hotly disputed issues that arose during the inquiry. It seems useful in these instances to let the committee speak for itself. The extracts which follow have not been selected to prove a case one way or another. They simply help to complete the picture of the investigation by reporting in the committee's own words its position on some of the points over which strongest controversy existed.

The final report devotes a large proportion of its space to an examination of Communist ideology for the purpose of showing its objectives and the intellectual, organizational, and procedural apparatus through which the party seeks to achieve these objectives. Extracts from official party publications are presented in carefully organized fashion in order to provide a documented account of Communist goals and methods of attaining them.[40]

This part of the committee report makes a worth-while contribution. It is presented in a matter-of-fact tone that avoids the sensational. Without attempting to editorialize, the committee permits the Communist Party to tell its own story: what it is for; what it is against; how it operates to achieve its ends; its attitude toward constitutional rights, social ethics, educational institutions, and so forth. Although the material presented is selected and arranged, it seems to give an accurate picture of Communist principles and methods. This section is informative and enlightening. Its purpose would have been more effectively achieved had the report been distributed widely—made available for general reading in the schools and by the public. Today the report seems particularly timely. Portions of it might well be reprinted and circulated extensively because they provide one of the best brief accounts of how Communists function. When the subject of communism and the schools is as important as it now is, information such as this would help people to clarify their own thinking.

To some readers this information will reveal conditions more sinister and dangerous than they had assumed. To others the threat of conspiratorial conquest will seem less ominous. But to everyone the problems posed by communism will be more concrete, less fanciful. In such an atmosphere the Ameri-

40 *Final Report,* pp. 24–178.

can answer to the threat of communism should be sought.

Other sections of the final report seem to have been written in a different spirit; they gave the impression of being less objective.

One of the most revealing segments of the committee's report is the page and a half devoted to the incident of the late S. J. Woolf, a distinguished artist and newspaper man who at that time was serving as a member of the Board of Higher Education by appointment of Mayor La Guardia.[41] The following excerpt, which represents the committee's entire comment upon the matter, is included here because it illustrates a note that recurs throughout the whole report. Mr. Woolf has no place in a report of this kind, but because he was brash enough to question some of the operating premises of the committee, this occasion to administer a public rebuke could not be resisted.

While on the subject of standards of conduct, it is necessary to refer to one instance on the part of a recently-appointed member of the Board of Higher Education which clearly calls for comment. We refer to the very remarkable concurring opinion filed by Mr. S. J. Woolf, as a member of the Trial Committee in the case of Philip S. Foner, one of the accused teachers, who was removed by the Board of Higher Education on the ground that he had been a member of the Communist Party at the City College, had participated in the preparation and circularization of the "Teacher-Worker," and had obstructed the work of the Legislative Committee by wilfully giving false testimony and withholding information.

Mr. Woolf, in a separate opinion, filed in November, 1941, concurred in recommending Foner's dismissal, saying: "In recommending the dismissal of Foner, I do so not because the prosecutor proved him to be a Communist, but because in doing this he also showed him to be a liar."

Our Committee does not criticize Mr. Woolf for this view. Mr.

41 *Ibid.*, pp. 339–340,

145

Woolf was entitled to conclude that the mere fact of Communism did not unfit Foner for service, if that represented Mr. Woolf's honest conviction after mature consideration of the facts.

The concluding paragraph of Mr. Woolf's opinion, however, raises a very different problem. After commenting on the testimony of the witnesses called on behalf of the Conduct Committee of the Board, which preferred the charges, and reaching the conclusion that they, and not Foner, had told the truth, Mr. Woolf wrote: "Foner a non-indoctrinating Communist was not a threat to the college. Foner, lying either through shame in his beliefs or to save his job, is as unfitted to remain a teacher as the informers who spoke to save theirs."

The Committee finds in these words an enunciation of a fundamentally improper standard of conduct. Mr. Woolf condemns the teachers whose testimony he believed because they did not commit perjury. His opinion is that persons who tell the truth under the compulsion of a subpoena and the sanction of an oath are by that mere fact disqualified for the public service.

Obviously, there is grave doubt as to whether a person who expresses such views in an official capacity is fit to hold public office. This would be true even in the case of an ordinary administrative department of the City or State. It is particularly true in the case of the schools, one of whose chief functions is to teach respect for the truth. Fulfillment of this function is necessarily jeopardized if such respect is lacking on the part of any member of the Board.

In the concluding section, when the committee makes suggestions and recommendations, the tone of the report becomes peremptory, threatening. Rather than attempt to paraphrase, some representative excerpts are reproduced.

Concerning Charles J. Hendley, president of the Teachers Union, the report observes:

The Committee does not charge that Mr. Hendley is a Communist, since it does not possess direct proof that he is. However, the Committee is not impressed by Mr. Hendley's professed ignorance of Communist influence in his Union. The Committee is conscious of Mr. Hendley's apparent lack of proper personal and professional standards, as evidenced by his unworthy conduct during the investigation and the things the Teachers Union has done under his leadership.

Mr. Hendley, however, still teaches. He still holds an office of honor and profit in the system he has constantly attacked and sought to discredit. And so far, it has not even been suggested by his employer, the Board of Education of the City of New York, that there is any question as to his fitness to continue in his position. Even this shocking case of conduct unbecoming a teacher was not sufficient to galvanize the Board of Education into action in the performance of its obvious duty. The public will look in vain for protection of the children against subversive influence as long as this attitude of inaction exists. We do not suggest that the Board has had any sympathy for Communism. We do find, however, a passive attitude which is almost equally dangerous.[42]

The Board of Education did not permit this statement to go unchallenged. On April 27, 1942, in a letter to the *New York Times,* James Marshall, president of the board, wrote that the board had taken no action against Hendley:

He is not accused by the Coudert committee of being a Communist. No witness has identified Mr. Hendley as a Communist.

In trials such as must be conducted by the Board of Education under the law to dismiss a teacher the evidence must be far greater than that which permits a legislative committee to bring charges. The evidence must be sufficient so that the judgment can withstand appeal to the State Commissioner or the courts.

The position taken in your editorial (April 24) that "we need not accept at face value the charge that the Board of Education or the Board of Higher Education, or any of their members, showed laxness in dealing with the Communist teachers" is eminently just. Statements to the contrary are without justification, for

[42] *Ibid.,* p. 354. Italics added.

147

within the financial means and the statutory powers the Board of Education has done its full duty. The public can well demand that in a time of national crisis reckless statements shall not be made to impugn the integrity of public officials or to cause our people to lose faith in their institutions.

The report of the Committee has done far more to break down American morale and the confidence of our people in American institutions than the handful of Communists in a system of more than 30,000 loyal teachers.[43]

In commenting upon the attitude of the educational authorities in New York City the report states:

Our Committee finds that the Board of Higher Education has acted creditably on the evidence presented at our public hearings. The Board on an earlier occasion sought unsuccessfully to trace the authorship of the "Staff" and "Teacher-Worker." There, however, the giving of credit must end. The Communist problem has existed in the schools for years. The attitude of both the Board of Education and the Board of Higher Education was, up to December, 1940, one of preferring to believe that the problem did not exist.

After conferring with the college authorities and also with the President of the Board of Education and the Superintendent of Schools, the Committee finds that both Boards were on adequate notice of the seriousness of the problem at all times. The fact of Communism in the schools has been continuously apparent for years. Communist shop papers were published both in the schools and in the colleges. The issue was constantly being agitated among the teachers. The Young Communist League was creating scenes of disorder and publishing subversive papers, especially in the high schools and colleges. In many schools, it was common knowledge that there was a definite line of cleavage between teachers who took their duties seriously and those belonging to Teachers Union "fractions" who used their schools as arenas for carrying on the "class struggle," to the intense annoyance, embarrassment

[43] *New York Times,* April 27, 1942.

148

and discomfort of their fellows. It was no secret from the school authorities that the Teachers Unions were disorderly organizations which were controlled by outside forces inimical to the schools. And when our investigating staff was organized, the problem of Communism forced itself on the Committee before the inquiry was two weeks old.

Yet the sad fact remains that no real effort to cope with the problem had originated with either the Board of Education or the Board of Higher Education. It is no answer that they lacked power or needed outside help, for they never asked for either. Whatever steps have been taken to protect the schools in the past proceeded from sources having no connection with the official bodies charged by law with the duty of protection. Unless, after a reasonable opportunity, there is a fundamental change in this respect, it will be incumbent on the Legislature to create new agencies for the task.[44]

One cannot fail to note the coercive flavor of the committee declaration.

Among the "non-legislative recommendations" the committee returns to the subject of the teachers' unions and persons belonging thereto:

Teachers who still belong to the former teachers' unions can no longer be deemed ignorant of the true nature or purposes of those organizations as secret and subversive political groups. Such teachers are either Communists, willing tools of Communism, or are wilfully blind to the record. Consequently, as a first step the Board of Education and the Board of Higher Education should ascertain the identity of those teachers who still belong to the former unions. Then a careful review of the conduct of each of these teachers should be undertaken. If such review is properly conducted, the Boards will be able to ascertain the identity of teachers whose continued employment is detrimental to the system.

In our judgment, the Board of Education should take immediate steps to fix responsibility for the performance of this work

[44] *Final Report,* pp. 355–356.

by detaching persons on the professional staffs from routine duties and assigning them to this task until its completion. They should be afforded adequate facilities for this work, and should be fortified with standing orders to all members of the teaching and administrative staffs to render full cooperation.

When this has been done, the Committee, so long as it is in existence, will render all proper and feasible aid to those in charge of the work. We are of the opinion that if it is once properly undertaken, the lines of its continuation will suggest themselves and much of value will be accomplished.

The assistance of the Committee will also be made available to the Board of Higher Education, which should immediately turn its attention to the members of the former College Teachers Union who continue to adhere to that organization. There are still individuals, especially at Brooklyn College, whose cases should be made the subject of careful study.[45]

Finally, the committee presents several recommendations for specific remedial legislation:

1. The enactment, as part of the Legislative Law, of civil penalties for refusal to give evidence before a Legislative Committee;
2. The enactment of an alternative disciplinary procedure in the City Colleges in harmony with the so-called democratization of the staffs, and the vesting of subpoena power in the Board;
3. The lengthening of the probationary period in the City Colleges from three to six years in the sub-professorial grades, with a permissive two-year period and a maximum three-year period in the case of original appointments to professorial rank;
4. The vesting of power in the Board of Education to appoint special examiners, with power of subpoena, to investigate the conduct of its employees and to act as trial examiners to be appointed from the regular professional staffs or otherwise, as the Board of Education may determine;
5. A Legislative declaration of the duty of Boards of Education and Higher Education to maintain adequate standards of conduct

[45] *Ibid.,* pp. 364–365.

as well as constant vigilance in ascertaining the facts relative to subversive activity in the schools, and a requirement of periodic reports to the Legislature on the discharge of such duty for at least the next two years.[46]

The Inconclusive Character of the Committee's Work

Perhaps the most striking thing about the Rapp-Coudert investigation is the inconclusiveness of its work. This statement may seem odd when the investigation resulted in the dismissal of twenty-four teachers, the resignation of eleven, and the failure to reappoint an indeterminate number of others. Unquestionably the inquiry brought results if measured by the number of persons purged. However, the investigation was conducted in order to ascertain "the extent to which, if any, subversive activities may have been permitted to be carried on in the schools and colleges of such educational system" [New York City]. The Coudert committee began with the public school system, shifted briefly to Brooklyn College, and ended with a more intensive screening of the faculty and staff of City College. In each instance the committee identified as Communists some members of the staffs of the institutions concerned and in each instance some removals occurred. In none of the three instances, however, was the committee successful in presenting a reasonably comprehensive report on the "extent of subversive activities" in the schools and colleges of New York City.

The reasons for this shortcoming were twofold. Subversive activity was never actually defined. Instead of facing this problem at the threshold of the inquiry, the committee assumed a priori that its chief assignment was that of locating Communists. This initial assumption seems unwarranted, but if one takes the committee upon its own terms, it still fell short of its goal. Through its work some Communists or alleged Com-

[46] *Ibid.*, pp. 363–364.

munists were brought to book. That is all. Whether the haul was a mere token or a full catch is not disclosed. The final report suggests that much remains to be done; the inquiring reader will agree. The extent of subversive activity (the number of Communists) in the schools is not reported.

IV

The Board of Higher Education

THE RAPP-COUDERT investigation cannot be separated from the train of events it set in motion. Although the action of the Board of Higher Education of New York City and that of the administrative officials of the municipal colleges may not strictly be classified as part of the legislative investigation, neither can they be regarded as unrelated. Board action followed and grew out of the findings of the Coudert committee. Moreover, in its first report the committee chided the educational authorities for their failure to recognize as a threat the acknowledged presence of Communists among the faculties and students and to take proper remedial measures. The committee went further and warned that unless the board and the administrative authorities did act the state legislature would take matters into its own hands.[1]

At least part of Senator Dunnigan's intention when he introduced his original resolution was that the boards of education and the administrative heads of the city educational institutions should be included among the subjects of investigation. This part of the inquiry was not pursued. Except for a brief review of the incidents preceding the departures of Presidents Robinson and Colligan, the subject went untouched along

[1] *Final Report,* Legislative Document (1942), No. 49, p. 356.

with most of the other items included in the legislative directive.

As the committee stated in its final report, it

did not conceive that its duty included the prosecution of or the preferment of removal charges against individual teachers or others. . . . The Committee's duty was to establish the extent and pattern of subversive activities in the schools. The exposure of individuals engaged therein was a necessary incident to the ascertainment of the pattern. Responsibility for appropriate action in the case of such individuals rested upon and was assumed by the Boards of Education and Higher Education.[2]

For some years preceding the inquiry the charge of Communist activities in the city schools had been made periodically. On one such occasion the Chairman of the Board of Higher Education had acknowledged the recurrent criticism:

Allegations of Communist activity in our city colleges are not news, nor is the fact of such activity unknown to our board. . . . Indeed, differences of opinion and attitude among faculty members are a wholesome sign of vitality, and as this is reflected in the teaching, it supplies students with a useful cross-section of the divergence of views in the community at large.[3]

Not all members of the Board of Higher Education agreed with this view. When the Coudert committee began its investigation and indicated that it had uncovered evidence of widespread Communist activity, the members of the board who had never been happy under the laissez-faire policy seized the opportunity to press for a change. They argued that unless the board acted expeditiously, it would be criticized, because public opinion was already demanding some official assurance that the board was not sympathetic to Communist infiltration in the schools.

There is little indication that this argument had great sub-

[2] *Ibid.*, p. 5.　　　　　　　　[3] *New York Times*, August 24, 1938.

stance because at this stage no public hearings had been held and most people simply were not aware of what was going on in the private hearings. Senator Coudert had communicated to the board the difficulties which his staff was encountering in its efforts to elicit information at the private hearings. Notwithstanding some difference of opinion among individual members, the Board of Higher Education adopted the following resolution on November 8, 1940:

Resolved that this Board extend to the Legislative Investigating Committee its full cooperation and that this Board record its judgment that all members of the faculties of the municipal colleges will and should assist the Committee in the accomplishment of the purposes stated in the Legislature's resolution creating the Committee.

This mild action did not satisfy Senator Coudert. On December 9, 1940, as the first public hearings were held, he called more insistently upon the board to use its authority in behalf of the committee. From this time on there actually was considerable discussion by the public of the Communist issue, although the more vocal element opposed rather than supported the inquiry. Nevertheless, the group on the board who demanded action against the offending teachers was in the stronger position. They could cite both public opinion and legislative disfavor as arguments in support of disciplinary proceedings looking toward the immediate ouster of all those who had been linked with communism.

On December 6, 1940, the Board of Higher Education adopted the following resolution:

Whereas, the Board of Higher Education, at its meeting of November 8, 1940, adopted the following resolution:
Resolved that this Board extend to the Legislative Investigating Committee its full cooperation and that this Board record its judgment that all members of the faculties of the municipal col-

leges will and should assist the Committee in the accomplishment of the purposes stated in the Legislature's resolution creating the Committee.

And Whereas, it has been reported in the public press that notwithstanding such resolution certain members of the staffs of the municipal colleges have refused to assist the Committee and to testify, now therefore be it

Resolved, That this Board request the Legislative Investigating Committee to submit to this Board such of the Minutes of the Legislative Investigating Committee as it deems proper together with such statement with reference to the subject matter which the Legislative Committee may deem proper and be it further

Resolved That the Chairman of this Board be authorized to request from the Corporation Counsel such opinion of the powers of this Board in respect to such refusal to testify.

And Be It Further Resolved, That a copy of this resolution be made available to the staffs of the colleges and to the public.

This resolution was precipitated by the refusal of twenty-five members of the Brooklyn College staff to testify at the private hearings conducted by one-man subcommittees and the subsequent action of the committee citing them for contempt.[4] On December 10, Ordway Tead, chairman of the Board of Higher Education, requested from William C. Chanler, city corporation counsel, a legal opinion as to the powers of the board in respect to the alleged refusal of the members of the Brooklyn College staff to testify. In his reply of December 11, Mr. Chanler stated:

The members of your staffs may not question the determination of the Board that they shall cooperate in full with the Legislative Committee. Accordingly, if any members of your staffs refuse to give full assistance to the Committee after having been advised of your determination they are guilty of insubordination. What disciplinary action should be taken is of course a question for your

4 See above, p. 89,

Board to decide. It is my opinion that dismissal upon charges under such circumstances would be upheld by the courts.[5]

The reluctance still entertained by some members of the board to commit themselves unreservedly until more of the facts were available is reflected in the second letter from Chairman Tead to Mr. Chanler on December 14. Prefacing his letter with the explanation that he did not believe that the latter had quite understood his previous request, Mr. Tead continued:

The Board would like to have your opinion as to whether or not the various teachers who refused to testify before the Committee had any legal basis for so doing sufficient to justify their refusal pending a determination of such rights by the courts.

You are aware, of course, of the action commenced by Professor Miner of Brooklyn College to obtain a determination of this and other related questions. In view of the pendency of this action and the question of deprivation of civil rights raised by the teachers involved, it would seem to me that it might be prudent for this Board to await the determination of the courts in this suit before taking any action in the matter.[6]

Two days later Mr. Tead announced publicly that the board was waiting for an opinion from the corporation counsel. He accompanied his announcement with the following statement:

The members of the Board of Higher Education share the deep concern of all right-minded citizens that no subversive activities shall go on in our colleges and that such actions, if they exist, shall be rooted out.

However, the Board is equally emphatic in its belief that one of the most important of the civil rights in the United States is that of recourse to legal tribunals. Since the question of the teachers in connection with the procedure used by the investigation is now before the courts, the overwhelming majority of the members of our Board believes that the rights of such teachers to seek

[5] Board of Higher Education files. [6] *Ibid.*

157

judicial determination should be safeguarded. For that reason we wish to make sure of the legal aspects involved in this matter.[7]

It is thus seen that in spite of considerable internal pressure from some of its own members the official position of the Board of Higher Education during the early stages of the investigation was one of sympathetic but restrained support rather than all-out advocacy. The board had yielded to the urgent demands of some of its members for action but it had acted with reserve. As the pressure became stronger—and most of it came from within rather than from without—the majority of the board moved to a less moderate position. Some of the chief mileposts in this shift will be noted.

On December 19, Charles H. Tuttle, a member of the board, wrote a long letter to Mr. Tead in which he surveyed the legal position of the board in relation to the recalcitrant teachers and reached the conclusion that the board had authority to remove them. He concluded, "I think that the public facts already known furnish an ample basis in law and in fact for further and effective action by the Board; and I am strongly of the opinion that the Board should not fail to keep the initiative in this vitally important matter." [8] From this time onward Mr. Tuttle never ceased in his efforts to move the board to institute ouster proceedings against all those named as Communists. His unwavering confidence in the soundness of his own position and his vigorous insistence upon action enabled him to exert considerable influence at this time. It is not to be inferred that other members of the board were by-passed or steam-rollered, or that they failed to exercise their own independent judgment. No such impression is intended. But Mr. Tuttle was outspokenly aggressive and he served as the focal point of those who agreed with him or whose uncertainty prevented their taking a strong stand against him.

[7] *Ibid.*   [8] *Ibid.*

In this particular instance Mr. Tuttle's insistence upon immediate punitive action was ineffectual. The day following his letter assuring that the board's legal power to remove was beyond question, the board's own legal counsel rendered a contrary opinion. Who was the better lawyer in this construction of the board's powers is not material. It is worthy of note, however, that in the removals which followed only one was taken in pursuance of the legal provisions cited in the letter.

Mr. Tead appointed a subcommittee headed by Lauson H. Stone to investigate the procedures employed at the private hearings and report back to the board with a further recommendation concerning the appropriate position for the board to take. While this subcommittee was prosecuting its own study, two events took place. On January 9, 1941, the legislature continued the Coudert committee and strengthened its investigative authority; on January 14, 1941, the committee adopted a resolution calling upon the boards and school authorities "to exercise their disciplinary powers in aid of any subpoena," etc.

On January 20, 1941, Mr. Stone's subcommittee reported back to the board that its investigation of the Coudert committee's private hearing procedure revealed no irregularities and that steps were being taken by the committee to formalize the safeguards already in use. The subcommittee further reported that it recommended no action against those teachers who had refused to appear, but it did propose the following resolution, which was approved and made public by the board:

Whereas the Legislature of the State in its 1941 session has indicated its intent that the Legislative Investigating Committee proceed with private hearings before a one-man subcommittee, as heretofore; and

Whereas, the Joint Legislative Committee has followed the policy of surrounding testimony taken on such private hearings with adequate safeguards for the protection of the witnesses appearing at such hearings and is now taking steps to formalize these safeguards;

Now Therefore, Be It Resolved, that this Board direct all members of the staffs and all other employees under its jurisdiction to promptly obey all subpoenas issued by the Joint Legislative Investigating Committee, and to give such testimony and such other information as may be required by the committee or any subcommittee thereof, and to otherwise cooperate with said committee to the best of their ability; and further

Resolved, that it will be the policy of the Board to take disciplinary action in accordance with law and its by-laws, for any failure to comply with the foregoing.

The Board Shifts to a More Aggressive Position

Everything suggests that up until the disclosure of several Communists among the faculties of the city colleges by Mr. Canning in early March, the board, although alerted to the imminence of the problem, had not permitted its more impetuous members to seize the bit. It had moved gradually but steadily from a position of passive acquiescence to the point where it had fully committed itself to active support of the inquiry; yet its temper remained moderate, its tone judicious.

After the Canning disclosures the board functioned in an atmosphere much more highly charged, and its demeanor became correspondingly less balanced. The counsel of moderation which had previously prevailed gave way before the group demanding more vigorous action. One senses that several members of the board, while out of sympathy with the current trend, acquiesced in silence or after only a mild demurrer because they felt that under the circumstances their objections would be misinterpreted. At any rate, as subsequent details will show, the board, for reasons that are not difficult to ascertain, acted with marked vigor in pursuance of the Rapp-Coudert disclosures. Whether it permitted itself to be jockeyed into an unnecessarily extreme position depends upon one's viewpoint.

On the day Mr. Canning named thirty-four members of the City College staff as Communists, Mr. Tuttle, the chairman of the Board of Higher Education's administrative committee for City College, informed the press that he would ask his committee to consider the immediate presentation of charges of "conduct unbecoming a teacher" against each of the thirty-four.[9] The following day the administrative committee voted unanimously to clear from the college any staff members "found to have aided, advocated, or propagated any subversive doctrine or activity or who have engaged in any unbecoming conduct." [10] Actually, this move was without legal significance because the administrative committee had no power to take such action. But the public did not know that Mr. Tuttle and his committee were merely "sounding off" without either authority or responsibility.

The haste with which the chairman acted is important for several reasons. As a lawyer he understood well the nature of the difference between an allegation and the kind of evidence necessary to convict or even to indict. Yet upon the unsupported statement of a single individual who had been known to speak inaccurately before, he urged bringing charges which might do irreparable harm to innocent individuals. There was slight possibility that he could have had the benefit of prior knowledge or additional information concerning the details upon which Mr. Canning's public statement was based. The statement itself was virtually barren of detail. It consisted of a single blunt declaration that the persons named had been fellow members of the party. Subsequently Mr. Canning was cross-examined in great detail by a subcommittee of the board. At that time he was able to supply many incidents which corroborated his earlier accusations against particular individuals but not against all those named. This information, however,

[9] *New York Times,* March 7, 1941, p. 12. The following day Mr. Canning named twenty additional members of the city school system as Communists.
[10] *Ibid.,* March 8, 1941, p. 1.

was not earlier available to the chairman because the Coudert committee declined to make its private testimony available to the board.[11]

On the same day that committee witness Canning testified, Morris U. Schappes, one of those named, also appeared. Mr. Schappes, one of the key leaders among the Communists at City College, had attempted to seize the strategic initiative by calling a press conference the previous day at which he admitted having been an active Communist but declared that he was no longer a member. Schappes' story both at the press conference and the committee hearing contained so many inconsistencies that it was patently false.[12] His perjury was so flagrant that he invited disciplinary action. The board would have been derelict in its duty had it not moved.

Lauson H. Stone, chairman of the board's conduct committee, announced that charges of "conduct unbecoming a member of the staff" would be brought against Schappes within a week.[13] Mr. Stone requested from Corporation Counsel Chanler an opinion as to the board's legal power to act against the teachers named.

The danger at this stage was that the testimony of Canning and Schappes made it easy to jump to hasty and ill-founded conclusions that everyone named was *ipso facto* guilty and should be removed. The action of the Taxpayers Union of New York City illustrates the kind of extreme reaction that usually accompanies a startling disclosure. The taxpayers' group called upon the mayor to eliminate ten million dollars from the budget for the city colleges and demanded that City College be closed until every un-American professor and student was removed. The message continued, "Unless you cooperate with us, we will institute a taxpayers' suit in the

[11] Letters from Senator Coudert to Lauson H. Stone, January 6, 8, 1941.
[12] *New York Times*, March 6, 1941, p. 23; March 7, pp. 1, 12.
[13] *Ibid.*, March 11, 1941, pp. 1, 11.

Supreme Court to curb subversive activities in city institutions." [14] Two days later, Joseph Goldsmith, president of the taxpayers' group, declared, "A majority of the students [in City College] are Communists and we are in favor of closing down the college until the situation is cleared up." [15]

It was especially important at this period that some responsible agency use its prestige in the direction of moderation rather than hysterical incrimination. The tendency to generalize from a single case to the conclusion that all members of the faculty and student body were inoculated with the virus of communism was the very sort of danger that the Board of Higher Education should have feared most and consequently have taken extra precautionary measures to prevent or neutralize.

Before it had had an opportunity to carry out any real inquiry into the details of the situation in the colleges, the board by a unanimous vote adopted the following resolution on March 7, 1941:

Resolved that it is the purpose of the Board of Higher Education not to retain as members of the collegiate staffs members of any Communist, Fascist or Nazi group or society, or to retain any individual, who, or member of any group which, advocates, advises, teaches or practices subversive doctrines or activities.[16]

Three days after the adoption of this resolution the member who had proposed it wrote Mr. Tead noting that the press comment had been unanimously favorable. He asked for a special board meeting so that he might introduce amendments to expedite removal in these cases.[17]

Despite a generally favorable editorial response in the New York press, the March 17 resolution attracted a growing vol-

14 *Ibid.*, March 9, 1941, p. 35.
15 *Ibid.*, March 10, 1941, pp. 1, 10.
16 *Ibid.*, March 18, 1941, p. 1.
17 Board of Higher Education files.

ume of adverse comment from educational institutions and organizations. Among others, the American Association of University Professors exhibited an interest which revealed deep concern over the meaning and effect of a resolution so sweeping in its language. While some members of the Board of Higher Education regretted that action had been taken so precipitately and looked about for some avenue of escape, an urgent minority stood by the resolution as literally interpreted, even though it could mean an outright repudiation of academic freedom.

After considerable discussion, the board resolved its differences by passing a new resolution on April 21, 1941:

Whereas, the Board of Higher Education has heretofore expressed its purpose not to retain as members of the collegiate staffs members of any Communist, Fascist, or Nazi group or society, or to retain any individual who, or members of any group which, advocates, advises, teaches or practices subversive doctrines or activities; and

Whereas, the Board deems it in the public interest to clarify the basis of its intended action in the case of any individual who, or member of any group which, advocates, advises, teaches, or practices subversive doctrines or activities, now therefore, be it

Resolved, that the Board considers it sufficient cause for dismissal of a staff member if he or she is proved (1) to have advocated, advised or taught the doctrine that the Government of the United States or of any state or political subdivision thereof should be overthrown or overturned by force, violence or any unlawful means or to be a member of any society or group of persons teaching or advocating such doctrine within the provisions of Section 12-a of the Civil Service Law; (2) to have engaged or participated in activities disruptive of the educational system, or to have accepted the obligations, standards or discipline of any group which requires its members to act in the interests of any foreign national group, or to follow any predetermined policy or course of conduct and further

164

Resolved, that it is the intention of the Board to adhere to its established policy not to discharge any member of its staffs (1) merely because of membership in a political organization unaccompanied by any of the activities or elements referred to in the resolution above or (2) merely because of any differences of opinion on political, economic or social matters.

The board's second effort, clearly an attempt to compromise the differences of the moderates and the extremists on and off the board, was neither brief nor clear. Instead of clarifying its basis of action—the declared purpose of the second resolution —it had produced a statement ambiguous enough to mean almost anything. Membership in a political organization was apparently permissible, provided such membership was unaccompanied by activities disruptive of the educational system, or acceptance of obligations, standards, or discipline of any group which requires its members to act in the interests of any foreign national group, or to follow any predetermined policy or course of conduct. These qualifications are vague because they are susceptible of varying interpretations. Whereas the original resolution carried an outright declaration that membership in the Communist Party was sufficient ground for disqualification as a teacher, the present resolution could be interpreted either way. It is difficult to see what purpose the resolution served, other than to provide an excuse for persons whose convictions were not very strong in the first place to declare that their original objections to the unequivocal language of the first resolution had been met.

The Board Begins Ouster Proceedings

On March 15, 1941, the conduct committee of the board preferred charges against Mr. Schappes. The four counts, which were elaborated by twelve typewritten pages of specifications, were: giving false and evasive testimony before the legislative committee; attempting to mislead and deceive the committee; editing a campus Communist publication which contained "coarse, abusive, scurrilous, scandalous and vulgar" attacks on college officials; attempting to implant Communist doctrines and principles in the minds of the students. Schappes was suspended by President Wright of City College upon receipt of the charges.

Morris Schappes was indicted for perjury three days later. Shortly thereafter he sued to enjoin further proceedings by the Board of Higher Education pending his trial on the perjury charge on the ground that his appearance before the board would prejudice his chances for a fair trial. After several weeks of legal fencing, he was sustained by the New York Court of Appeals, although his supplementary plea that the trials of other teachers before the Board of Higher Education also be stayed pending his own court trial was denied.[18]

With the Schappes case temporarily suspended, the college authorities had turned to other cases. On March 20, 1941, Dr. Lewis Balamuth, an instructor of physics, was dropped from the roster of evening session teachers. All appointments to the evening session were temporary, hence no formal removal proceedings were necessary. Since Dr. Balamuth did enjoy tenure in the day session, he could be removed from this position only

---

[18] The perjury indictment specified four counts on which Schappes had given false testimony: (1) that there were only four members of the Communist unit on the City College campus and that he was the only one from 1938 through 1939; (2) that he had lied about the *Teacher-Worker,* the Communist publication at City College; (3) that he knew no other Communist who was a member of either the Teachers Union or the College Teachers Union; and (4) that there was no Communist faction in either union. After some delay Schappes was tried in June, 1941. He was found guilty on all four counts and sentenced to one and a half to two years' imprisonment. Appeal on the case dragged on for two years, when the New York Court of Appeals sustained the lower court verdict in July, 1943. Chief Judge Lehman filed a dissenting opinion stating that while the evidence indicated that the defendant gave false testimony, there was not enough evidence to sustain a finding of guilt of perjury in the first degree.

through the formal action of preferring charges and trial. It is interesting and probably significant that such charges were not brought against Mr. Balamuth at this time. He had not yet appeared before the Coudert committee in public hearing; neither had any of the others who had been named by Mr. Canning. On March 22, Maxwell N. Weisman, another of the persons named by Canning, was removed from his position as executive director of the House Plan of City College, the college social center. As in the case just mentioned, this position did not carry tenure, but he was not suspended from his position as tutor of English, where he did enjoy tenure.

Both of these individuals had many years of effective service in their respective positions. Both had won recognition for their work. In neither case was there any suggestion that their efficiency had deteriorated in any way so as to justify separation. They were simply cut adrift.

No one can challenge the legal authority of the college administration in removing these two men. But by taking such full advantage of the technicalities of the law, the administration invited speculation as to its motives. The only evidence it could have had at the time this action was taken was circumstantial, fragmentary, based entirely on the unsupported statements of a single individual. No effort had been made to question those accused; nor had they been given an opportunity to reply. What would have been sacrificed by postponing removal until enough of the facts were in to justify formal preferring of charges and suspension? For the college administration's heavy reliance upon a legal technicality, there could be only two possible explanations. Either its hand had been forced or it had lost its own sense of judicious procedure. In either case such official reaction at the threshold of this difficult period was anything but reassuring.

The first of the public hearings before the Rapp-Coudert committee at which the accused teachers appeared was held on

March 24. Taken in alphabetical order, six teachers testified. At intermittent meetings of the committee running on into June, the remaining teachers who had requested to be heard appeared. In addition, the committee tried unsuccessfully to induce seven teachers who had not requested a public hearing to take the stand and declare whether or not they were party members. When the individuals refused to take the stand, committee counsel read into the public record excerpts from the transcript of the private testimony in which they had testified under oath that they were not Communists.

At varying intervals, after each person had appeared at the committee's public hearings, charges were brought against him by the Board of Higher Education committee and he was suspended.[19] The first case following that of Schappes was Arthur Braunlich, Jr., tutor in English. The procedure followed in his case established the general pattern for those to follow. Braunlich appeared before the Coudert committee on March 24. On March 25 charges were preferred against him by the conduct committee of the board; the following day he was suspended by President Wright. Mr. Wright issued a memorandum to all members of the instructional staff in which he explained the basis for his action and the reasons lying behind it. The pertinent parts of the memorandum follow:

In connection with this action, I should like to make clear to the staff the general policy that I am following.

In the first place, the suspension should not be construed as a prejudgment of the case. Rather, it is a recognition of the seriousness of the charges that have been preferred, and of the proprieties of the situation: If a person against whom serious charges are preferred were to continue in the classroom, inevitably a distracting element would be introduced which would affect the

[19] The direct connection between appearance at public hearing and suspension has already been noted. See above, p. 109.

students as well as the teacher, no matter how disinterested and objective he might try to be. In addition, the suspension enables the accused person to give his full time to the preparation of his defense. Nor is any loss of salary necessarily involved, for if the accused person is exonerated by decision of the Board, he is entitled to receive the salary of which he was deprived during the period of suspension.

It should be pointed out that the by-laws of the Board are designed to insure a fair trial and to give full protection to the accused person, including the option of a preliminary hearing by the Faculty Committee on Personnel, the right of representation by counsel at his trial before the Board Committee, the right to examine and cross-examine witnesses and to produce witnesses on his own behalf, and the further right of appeal from the trial committee before final determination by the Board.

The Trials

The first person actually to be tried by the Board of Higher Education was John K. Ackley, registrar of City College. Charges were preferred against him on March 28. He made formal reply to the charges on April 21. He was tried by a three-man committee of the board on June 9–12; found guilty by the committee on June 25. After a public hearing before the Board of Higher Education on June 30, he was found guilty and dismissed. With minor variations the procedure in the cases of all those dismissed on charges followed this same pattern. In all, twenty persons were tried, found guilty, and dismissed. Eleven resigned apparently to avoid dismissal.

Before discussing the charges preferred against individual teachers and the trials upon these charges, it seems desirable to pause for a brief explanation of the pertinent laws and regulations affecting tenure and removal. The law provided that persons having tenure—teachers with the rank of tutor and above—might be removed or suspended for one or more of the following reasons:

a. incompetent or inefficient service
b. neglect of duty
c. physical or mental incapacity
d. conduct unbecoming a member of the staff. This provision shall not be so interpreted as to constitute interference with academic freedom.

The law further provided that proceedings for removal should be conducted in accordance with the by-laws of the board and guaranteed a public hearing before the board or a committee thereof with charges stipulated and with full opportunity to be represented by counsel. In the event that the initial hearing was held before a committee of the board, the accused was entitled to a further public hearing before the entire board, again with the privilege of counsel. Pending his trial, any person against whom charges had been made could be suspended by the president of the college, with the concurrence of the department head. If the person so suspended desired, he might request that the charges be submitted to a faculty committee for consideration. In this case the initial hearing would be held before the faculty committee and the board hearing would be postponed pending the report of the faculty committee.

None of the persons suspended requested hearings before faculty committees. Some defenders of board action have interpreted this failure to employ the faculty committee trial procedure as an admission by the accused that they did not have good cases. Inquiry among members of the college faculties on both sides of the issue suggests that this is not a fair interpretation of the situation. The faculties of the colleges were not active participants in the controversy; with a very few exceptions, the members of the faculty did their utmost to avoid being implicated on one side or the other. There would have been great reluctance to serve on such a committee for reasons which seem quite obvious. The issue was plainly between the administration and the accused teachers. The faculty as a whole wanted no part in the battle.

So far as the accused teachers were concerned, the same opinion prevailed. Since the board was their accuser, they saw little point in prolonging their uncertain status by interposing an extra step in their campaign for reinstatement. Their decision to take their cases directly to the administration seems logical, but has no bearing upon the merits of their cases, one way or another.

One may wonder at the passive role played by the college faculties. Actually a number of individual teachers did come to the defense of those named by the Coudert committee. Several signed statements testifying to the good character of their colleagues. Others appeared as character witnesses during the trial committee proceedings. Earlier reference has been made to the Brooklyn College instructors who voiced disapproval of investigating committee procedures. On the whole, however, the faculties were singularly quiescent. A few teachers resented the excesses of some of the extremely militant Communists and felt that they were willfully jeopardizing the real interests of the teachers by their party tactics. This group felt that it was necessary that the faculty as a whole should be cleared of the stigma of communism; they regarded the investigation as the best available agency for carrying out this task and were not inclined to interfere with its work. On the contrary, many of them co-operated willingly with the committee and later with the Board of Higher Education. There is some indication that in retrospect some of these individuals feel that they might better have followed a different course. Others, however, express the view that they would act no differently if a similar situation arose again.

Most of the faculties of the city colleges simply remained aloof from the investigation and its aftermath. Among this group the general attitude was that it was none of their affair and they did not wish to become involved. Many who had sympathy with the individuals named and who disliked the activities of the investigating committee did not feel they could afford the risk of being implicated by voicing their disapproval. They played safe by remaining silent.

In every case trials were conducted by special trial committees. Although a number of different board members served on the committees, procedure varied but little. Almost constant legal fencing by counsel for the board and the teacher was a regular feature of each trial. Various members of the board who were lawyers presided, and with a single exception they exhibited conspicuous effort to be fair, frequently ruling in favor of the person under charges.

In this first instance, the chairman frequently slipped over into the role of prosecutor. For him the issue had already progressed beyond the stage of conjecture—the question of guilt apparently no longer remained open. His conduct of the first trial must be considered in this framework. No matter how conscientiously he may have striven to be fair, he did not wholly succeed because he could not divorce himself from the case. Although he occupied the position of judge, he could not disassociate himself from the post of counsel.

Certainly, in reading the record of the first trial, the impression is quickly established that the defendant's case is hopeless. Unless the transcript presents a distorted picture of the trial itself, the proceeding was prejudiced and the verdict hardly in doubt. Subsequent trials took place in an atmosphere quite different, but the effects of this first one could not be wholly ignored. The reasons for this lay in the nature of the proceedings themselves and the type of evidence produced.

In each case brought up for trial the charges were substantially the same: membership in the Communist Party, hence perjury for having denied such membership while under oath; failure to co-operate with the legislative investigating committee after being directed to do so by the Board of Higher Education; participation in Communist activities in the college, hence neglect of duty. Although friends of the board insisted that the fact of membership in the Communist party was not in itself the ground on which teachers were actually tried and removed, their arguments are hardly convincing.

In the first place, the board resolution of March 17, 1941, had declared categorically that "it is not the purpose of the Board of Higher Education to retain as members of the collegiate staffs members of any Communist, Fascist or Nazi group." The more moderate language of the April 21st resolution had not rescinded this declaration. At the first trial much of the questioning, especially that part conducted by the chairman of the trial committee, was plainly directed at this point: extensive cross-examination as to the beliefs of the accused, the books which he had read, the publications he followed and his views on recent events such as the Russian invasion of Finland. This line of questioning may have been relevant to the question of his party membership, but it had no bearing on the other charges.

Once the question of party membership was settled affirmatively, the other charges followed almost automatically. The issue of perjury grew directly out of party membership; failure to co-operate with the legislative committee and neglect of duty were also clearly bound up with this same point. Whether or not the board voted to dismiss a teacher on the ground of being a Communist, it seems evident that he would not have been removed if he could have proved that he was not a party member. The other charges would not have been pressed. It was not necessary to prove conclusively that the individual had been guilty of conduct justifying dismissal separate and apart from being a Communist.

For those who actually were party members their conduct *after* the investigation started certainly could be interpreted by the board as ground for dismissal. Deliberate, premeditated lying under oath, if clearly established, would seem sufficiently reprehensible to fall within the fourth ground for removal: conduct unbecoming a teacher.

Whether the motive for such cold-blooded perjury was sub-servience to a superior command, conspiratorial agreement, or simply repudiation of ordinary ethical standards, any teacher who consciously and deliberately chose to lie under these circumstances disqualified himself in the eyes of the board to remain as a teacher.

The Dilemma Faced by the Teacher Under Charges

In a sense such a teacher was placed in a dilemma from which there was no escape. By its decision that party member-ship disqualified a teacher, the Board of Higher Education had forced its employees to lie if they hoped to keep their jobs. No matter how sincerely a teacher might believe that his party membership had not interfered with his teaching, and, no matter how innocent his affiliation, he would never be given an opportunity to present his case on its own merits. In order to qualify for anything resembling an unbiased hearing, he had to plead nonmembership at the very beginning.[20]

[20] For the person falsely charged with belonging to the Communist Party, the situation was equally ironic. One of the dismissed teachers interviewed in the course of this study, a scientist who was subsequently investigated and cleared for classified work by the United States Navy, was called in by his de-partment head and the president of the college and told that if he would admit his party membership he would be retained. When he remonstrated that he could not make such an admission truthfully, he was dropped without trial be-cause he did not have tenure.

This is the only case encountered in which persons in positions of authority indicated that an admission of party membership would not be tantamount to automatic dismissal. There is no sure way of knowing whether anyone who ad-mitted a Communist affiliation would actually have been retained. Neither the board nor the college administration publicly took a position on this point ex-cept in the March 17 resolution and its equivocal supplement of April 21. One feels that the temper of the period in which the ouster proceedings occurred was not such as to be reassuring to any teacher who might have contemplated such action.

The evidence indicates that these mutually unsatisfactory alternatives faced many individuals whose personal situations differed greatly. Although each case was unique, at least three fairly well-defined groups are discernible: those who were out-and-out Communists consciously and ruthlessly following the line and playing the game without scruple or reservation; those who had joined the party and were technically Communists but who either had never become ardently committed or who had regretted their earlier action and were seeking an escape; those who had never joined the party but who had been caught up in the Coudert committee's net because of their activity in some of the organizations intimately associated with the party.

So far as the first group is concerned, they had joined the party presumably after full consideration of the issues at stake and of the possible hazards involved. Whether or not their party activity had in the past been truly "subversive" in the sense that they had deliberately abused their positions to indoctrinate students or had engaged in conspiratorial, destructive action, their conduct during the hearings and after did raise serious questions as to their continued eligibility to remain as teachers. They had made a considered choice even though they knew that perjury, if proved, would undoubtedly result in their dismissal; they were now called upon to face the consequences of their own actions.[21] For the second group

[21] Oddly enough neither the Coudert committee nor the Board of Higher Education showed any relish for placing chief emphasis upon the fact of telling the truth, although this point along with other things was in effect covered in the vague phrase "conduct unbecoming a teacher." In the case of one trial, however, a member of the trial committee created quite a sensation when he stated that he was voting to dismiss the teacher concerned, not because he was proved to be a Communist, etc., but because he was a liar. The board member offended the committee and the board by adding that in his opinion the teachers who had confessed their previous party membership but who were now co-operating with the investigation were equally disqualified because they had lied also. Apparently this point of view was offensive to the Coudert committee because

the situation was somewhat different. They were reluctant Communists, or, at worst, nominal, passive ones. Had they been given an opportunity to confess their "error" without prejudice, some of them would have been only too happy for a way out. Among this group were several who were certainly no more culpable than those former party members who had given state's evidence against their former comrades. The only difference was one of chronology. Had the attitude and procedure of the board been different, it is at least arguable that several of this group would have been salvaged. Even if one ignores the personal considerations applicable to this group, the conclusion seems inescapable that the individuals concerned had been virtually forced into a choice which led to dismissal and ostracism in their profession. A number of this group were superior persons of proved capacity. The loss to the school system outweighed the personal loss.

It is with respect to the final group that real injustice was done, however. The number of persons in this group was not large. Some of those associated with the investigation and trials have observed that their value more than counterbalanced the few hardships that may have resulted. The point overlooked by those who take this position is that other procedures might have achieved equally salutary results without the adverse effect. The vice of the procedure employed was its emphasis upon party membership. Once this charge had been directed at a person, he was in a very weak position because there was no practical way in which he could refute it. Membership was not proved in some of these cases because proof was not available. But neither was it disproved for the same reason.

The evidence presented no sure case one way or the other.

---

in its final report the incident is given considerable attention and the tone is firmly reproving. See above, p. 145.

In order to review the evidence and reach a verdict one had to operate upon certain premises and make certain assumptions. The pattern set in the first trial was followed in subsequent proceedings, despite the fact that the later trial committees exhibited a more judicious attitude. Accordingly, each committee approached each case independently but with certain assumptions already established. They tended to examine the facts of each case, but the factual records were amazingly similar and it is not surprising that they reached the same conclusions.

As time went on, various members of the board had an opportunity to discuss the cases with other people. They discovered points of view and aspects with which they had not been familiar. They found occasion to re-examine some of their own assumptions and discovered that their earlier views were subject to revision. It is not without significance that in the Withrow case, not settled until almost two years after the first charges had been brought, the trial committee voted to acquit. This decision was approved by the board, although the member who had earlier been instrumental in shaping board policy, joined by three others, voted against acquittal. He stated for the record that in his opinion the evidence was more than sufficient to sustain conviction.[22] Had the evidence changed or had the attitude of the board changed?

Another instance which grew out of quite different circumstances sheds further light upon the interpretation of the evidence presented in the cases here under consideration. In the only case where the decision of the Board of Higher Education has been subjected to review by another agency, the board was not sustained. Francis J. Thompson, an instructor in City College, was tried on the usual charges in May, 1942. On November 23, 1942, the trial committee reported to the board that the charges had been supported by the evidence

[22] Board of Higher Education, *Minutes*, March 15, 1943.

adduced at the trial. The committee recommended dismissal. Because Mr. Thompson entered military service, the board postponed final action. After his honorable discharge from the military·service in November, 1946, the case was argued before the board. On December 16, 1946, the board formally approved the report of the trial committee and dismissed Thompson.[23]

Mr. Thompson appealed his case to the Commissioner of Education. On December 23, 1947, the Acting Commissioner of Education sustained the appeal and ordered Thompson's reinstatement with back pay. The opinion ruled that under the existing state law membership in the Communist Party was not grounds for dismissal. The most significant part of the opinion, however, is that section which deals with the conclusiveness of the evidence presented against the accused:

The second two charges [obstructing the legislative committee by willfully giving false and evasive testimony at the hearings, and violating the board's resolutions of January 20, 1941, by giving false and evasive testimony and withholding information within his knowledge while testifying before the committee] are premised upon appellant's giving false testimony to the effect that he was not a member of the Communist Party. There is no evidence in the record that the appellant ever had a card of membership in the Communist organization or has paid any dues thereto. While the testimony and record are voluminous, the conclusion of the Board that he was a member of this party is based primarily on the claim of two persons who allege they saw him in attendance at a "unit meeting." There is no claim that he has ever in his teaching or at meetings or other occasions advocated the principles of the Communist Party.

He denies that he has ever been a member or that he was present at the meetings noted. I am not convinced from my examina-

[23] Presumably the board considered the case against Thompson stronger and more serious than that against Withrow.

178

tion of the record that he was present on these occasions. In any event, in the absence of evidence of actual membership or that he has, by his professional attitude or teaching, indicated his acceptance of its doctrines, it does not seem to me that, even though it be established that he was present at these meetings, this fact in itself would be sufficient to predicate a conclusion that he was a member of the Communist Party.

Other claims as to his connection with this organization seem to me to be primarily inference without sufficient objective bases to establish this relationship. While I conclude that the Board of Higher Education was justified in giving consideration to this case, it is my view, after a most careful perusal of the entire record, that the evidence is insufficient to establish that he was a member of the Communist Party.[24]

The Acting Commissioner also noted in his decision that the appellant, Thompson, had served in army intelligence from January, 1943, to November, 1946, and had received an honorable discharge. "His connection with the intelligence branch of the services would seem to indicate that the Army had no occasion to believe that his philosophies of life were inimical to the interests of the United States."

The board's effort to reopen the case was denied by the Commissioner of Education on August 31, 1948, on the ground that no new material evidence had been submitted.

It would be dangerous to attempt to draw decisive conclusions from this lone case, but it raises interesting questions. The charges against Thompson were the same as those brought against most of the other teachers. The evidence assembled against him was fully as extensive and complete as that which resulted in conviction and dismissal of several other teachers.

[24] University of the State of New York, the State Department of Education, Before the Commissioner, *In the Matter of the Appeal of Francis J. Thompson from the Action of the Board of Higher Education of the City of New York*, December 23, 1947.

Yet in the one instance where this evidence was reviewed by an outside agency, it was ruled not sufficient to justify dismissal. What would have been the result if all of the board's decisions had been reviewed? One can only speculate.

The question immediately arises, why were there not more appeals from the board's action? Actually, there were a great many. Immediately following their dismissal, sixteen instituted appeals in the New York Supreme Court, but the cases were never argued. Discussion with individuals involved and with their legal counsel indicates that the main reason for failure to press the appeal was financial. None of the individuals had sufficient financial resources to fight an appeal in which the chances of ultimate victory were so uncertain. Another factor added further complications. Many of the teachers involved in these cases were already being drawn into the military service, and this furnished another reason for postponing their appeals. Even should they decide to press their cases, they could not hope to obtain a final answer before being inducted into military service.

There was no disposition on the part of the Board of Higher Education to push for a judicial review of its action. The office of the corporation counsel of New York City exhibited even less enthusiasm. The attorney who served as counsel for the teachers in their trials before the board has indicated that technically the appeals are still pending because the city legal officers have never filed a reply. He himself has not pushed the appeals because at the termination of the war and the return to civilian life of his clients most of them preferred to let the matter drop.

They were absorbed in the problems of re-establishing their interrupted lives and did not feel that they had either the time or money to divert to a project which was so far behind them and so uncertain in its results. The general feeling was a desire to forget the incident, to wipe out the painful memory rather than to revive it with all the disagreeable publicity that would inevitably be involved.

For its part, the Board of Higher Education was content to let the matter rest, having no desire to reopen the controversy. When the Thompson decision went against it, the board quickly made a quiet financial settlement because it feared that wide publicity might encourage a general move to revive the entire issue.

There seems little likelihood that anything will be done at this late date. The accident of the war coming just at the time it did undoubtedly prevented the actions and procedures of the Board of Higher Education from being subjected to careful judicial scrutiny. However idle it is to speculate upon what the courts would have done, it is regrettable that they were not permitted this opportunity. As it is, neither the board nor its critics can know whether the procedures employed in these crucial cases were such as to meet judicial standards of due process. This loss is especially serious because of the likelihood that similar cases will become increasingly common in the future.

The Board's Procedures Reviewed

The Board of Higher Education was attacked from several quarters for the actual procedures it employed in the cases of the teachers named as Communists. The Teachers Union, particularly its Committee to Defend Public Education, outdid all other groups in the volume and shrillness of its attack. In the *New York Teacher* of June, 1941, David Goldway released a blast which is fairly representative of the tone regularly employed:

Meanwhile, the Board of Higher Education, servile lackey of the Coudert Committee, pounces on the victims prepared by the Windels inquisition, levels wholesale charges against them, and has them summarily suspended. In its zeal, it brushes aside its own by-laws and even violates the state tenure law. It makes a mockery of academic freedom and pours terror and hysteria into its colleges. It obsequiously tenders to Mr. Windels full power to dictate the employment and dismissal of staff members.[25]

Criticism, more temperate but no less severe, was voiced by the Committee for Democracy and Intellectual Freedom. The American Civil Liberties Union and the American Association of University Professors likewise expressed apprehension concerning the procedures of the board. To these must be added numerous individual communications from prominent figures in the educational world.

The chief criticism directed against the board was that its procedures were arbitrary and that it depended too fully upon the disclosures of the Coudert committee rather than upon its own independent investigation for evidence to sustain the disciplinary measures which it took against the accused teachers. This is the essence of the charges made by Mr. Goldway and the same point was stressed by the Committee for Democracy and Intellectual Freedom. This charge does not stand up under close examination, however; the board exercised diligence in its efforts to ferret out the facts, although, paradoxically, the majority of its members can take no credit.

A small but insistent minority on the board resisted the tendency to judge by formula that has already been described. This group hammered away on the point that only by detailed factual investigation would it be possible to determine whether the persons publicly named were actually Communists and, more important, whether the activities in which they had engaged should actually be adjudged subversive. Through the insistence and actual intervention of this group, a board committee did engage in extensive investigation on

[25] Page 17.

its own. For the most part these investigations were carried on behind the scenes with no publicity at the time and no subsequent announcement so that the general public was not apprised of their ever having taken place. Two cases are illustrative.

After the public statement concerning Communist activities in Brooklyn College, a committee of the board held extensive private hearings at which it interviewed fifteen members of the Brooklyn College staff. The group was a representative cross section of the college faculty. Some had been named as Communists, others were suspected of being implicated, still others had not been identified or even mentioned in connection with the inquiry. Each individual was questioned in detail on conditions and activities in the college. Interrogation as revealed by the stenographic transcript, though careful, searching, persistent, was conducted on a level that was moderate and considerate. Much information not previously divulged in public hearings and therefore not previously available to the board was turned up in this hearing.[26]

On another occasion, after Mr. Canning had made his public statements, in the course of which he named fifty-four alleged Communists, he was invited to appear for a private hearing before a committee of the board. At this session, held on March 22, 1941, he was pressed to elaborate in much greater detail his previous testimony. Members of the committee probed deeply for specific evidence to support the general charges made at the public hearings. Presumably he had also mentioned these names at the private sessions of the Coudert committee.

Both the Coudert committee and the Board of Higher Education are entitled to credit for the care exercised in withholding names. Nevertheless some persons may have been publicly named as Communists when they were not. Errors of this kind

[26] Board of Higher Education files, no date given.

are probably unavoidable when identification is determined by sworn statement unsupported except by circumstantial evidence. Numerous borderline cases occur where the preponderant evidence strongly suggests that a particular individual is a party member. In several such instances, especially in the Coudert committee rather than before the Board of Higher Education, it now seems likely that innocent persons were unjustly implicated. This, of course, is one of the worst vices of this kind of inquiry. In the very nature of things, suspicion tends to become conviction because doubts are usually resolved against the suspected person.

Except for this type of error, which may be regarded as an operational characteristic, the committee and the board scrupulously avoided the reckless smearing of innocent individuals that accompanied the Lusk and McNaboe investigations. Both the committee and the board, in the course of private hearings, were given the names of persons whom witnesses identified as Communists, but who were never formally charged. Although their instruments of verification were clumsy and in some instances inaccurate, both the committee and the board distinguished allegation from guilt and strove to preserve this distinction in their work. In its final report the committee stated that it had in its files information tending to implicate 434 others in addition to the 69 whom it identified publicly. Under less responsible leadership the committee might easily have dragged many of these names into the muck.

Careful attention to detail and conscientious search for specific evidence was not confined to the pretrial phase of the Board of Education's handling of the cases. Each person against whom formal charges were preferred was accorded a trial in which he had full opportunity to present his case: legal counsel, full opportunity to cross-examine opposition witnesses, and unrestricted privilege of summoning witnesses in his own behalf were granted each person, and no effort was

184

made to abridge proceedings. Trials usually ran into several days with the stenographic record totaling three hundred to four hundred pages.

In retrospect the board's handling and disposition of the Communist cases is not reassuring, notwithstanding the favorable points that have been mentioned. When the episode is viewed as a whole, the record suggests that the board was more intent on sloughing off an embarrassing problem than of thinking it through. It failed to establish a policy which could be defended from the standpoint of democratic institutions and upon the basis of genuine academic freedom. Apparently it lacked the courage to adhere to high principles while it considered the cases of the individual teachers named by the Coudert committee.

The board's error did not lie in its failure to employ procedures adequate to the occasion, except in the relatively minor instances already discussed. Its real shortcoming, in the writer's opinion, was its timorous acceptance of the Coudert committee's conception of subversive activity without serious inquiry or discussion. The activities being carried on by the Teachers Union and other organizations were annoying, frequently extremely irritating. But most of the objectives which the union was working for were reasonable or at least understandable. Better pay, expanded facilities, greater retirement benefits, and so forth, are not subversive goals, nor do they fall within the category of dangerous and revolutionary doctrines. Even on the peace front—a point made much of by those who stressed the Communist threat—by no means all persons who vigorously opposed war during this period were either Communists or Communist tools. Many patriotic Americans, untainted by the slightest breath of communism, entertained this view.

The board swallowed the committee's own questionable definition of subversive activity without more than a fleeting tremor. Once this had occurred, there was nothing left for it to do but put its machinery of prosecution in motion. Its meticulous procedure was a poor substitute for the courageous facing up which should have preceded it.

V

The Feinberg Law

P ROTECTIVE" legislation, a characteristic feature at
   every legislative session at Albany in recent years, expanded markedly in 1949. The legislative temper reflected a
note not confined to New York State or the eastern seaboard.
During preceding months numerous disclosures had given
some indication of Communist activity upon a wide front.
The federal loyalty program had provided many headlines
and there was a general air of uneasiness and insecurity. The
period was one in which frightened people cast about for
protective devices, either unaware or indifferent to the fact
that additional laws would give them no greater feeling of
security than those already in existence. It is noteworthy that
those who press most vigorously for additional legal restrictions derive the least sense of protection from each new law
and thus are obliged to seek ever more sweeping repressive
measures.

Fear was in the air during the 1949 session of the New York
Legislature; it was revealed in the number and extreme sever-
ity of the bills introduced. But other forces also contributed
directly to the climate of opinion in which the Feinberg Law
was sired.

The legislature had long harbored a smoldering resentment
against the educational authorities. State legislative bodies

always seem to provide fertile breeding grounds for epidemics of suspicion and repression toward the schools. New York State is certainly no exception. As earlier sections of this report have illustrated, the legislature has not required very much priming to renew its attacks upon the teacher.

When the Rapp-Coudert committee rendered its final report, it took considerable pains to record its disappointment at the laxity of school officials:

Yet the sad fact remains that no real effort to cope with the problem [Communism in the schools] had originated with either the Board of Education or the Board of Higher Education. It is no answer that they lacked power or needed outside help, for they never asked for either. Whatever steps have been taken to protect the schools in the past proceeded from sources having no connection with the official bodies charged by law with the duty of protection. *Unless, after a reasonable opportunity, there is a fundamental change in this respect, it will be incumbent on the legislature to create new agencies for the task.*[1]

The committee went on to recommend certain procedural changes designed to expedite disciplinary action against subversive teachers. It included as its final proposal a requirement that periodic reports to the legislature on the discharge of such duty should be made by school authorities during at least the next two years.[2]

Legislative attention was diverted from the Communist issue by the time the report was received. None of the Coudert committee's recommendations was enacted into law and the New York City boards of education were chiefly concerned with lowering the curtain on the Communist episode. The issue of communism in the schools was permitted to lapse, but its eclipse was only temporary; those in the legislature who had

[1] *Final Report*, Legislative Document (1942), No. 49, p. 356. Italics added.
[2] *Ibid.*, pp. 363-364.

been most insistent in the demand for a purge of subversives had neither lost interest nor changed their views. Nor had they been gratified by the way the educational authorities had terminated their drive against dangerous teachers.

There was on the part of one segment of the legislature a tendency to believe that its will had been flaunted by those administering the schools: legislative intent had been sabotaged by administrative inaction. At least part of the sentiment behind the drive for more severe legislation in 1949 stemmed from a desire to force more vigorous enforcement of laws already on the books.

But there was still another element in the legislative state of mind which produced the Feinberg Law. The Thompson case, already discussed, provided the immediate and direct stimulus. The decision in that case, it will be recalled, ruled that under existing law membership in the Communist Party was not sufficient ground for disqualification as a teacher. To block legislative loopholes revealed by the Thompson decision and to force administrative action were thus the primary objectives of the Feinberg Law.

The statute itself, the latest in the steadily growing list of New York legislative responses to the recurrent alarums over subversive forces, can best be understood and appraised against the background of similar proposals introduced earlier in the 1949 session. The Mauhs bill, introduced in the Assembly on February 7, 1949, proposed to amend Section 2523 of the state education law by adding a new subdivision 15:

Any person who is a member of the Communist Party, or who refuses to disclose upon inquiry whether or not he is a member of the Communist Party, or who subscribes to its doctrine shall be ineligible for employment in the teaching profession or in the school systems in this state.[3]

[3] Assembly Int. 1488, Nos. 1530, 3308.

Although the New York City Board of Education went publicly on record as favoring the Mauhs bill with slight amendments, the Assembly did not act.[4] Shortly thereafter, companion bills were introduced in both chambers by Senator Charles V. Scanlon and Assemblyman Frank J. McMullen to require of all persons employed by the state an additional loyalty oath as follows: "I am not a member of the Communist Party or affiliated with such party. I do not believe in and I am not a member of or support any organization that believes in or teaches the overthrow of the United States government by force or illegal or unconstitutional methods." [5] Also introduced were companion bills to make membership in the Communist Party the basis of ineligibility for appointment or election to public office.[6] The public oath bill received no action in either chamber; the Assembly passed by a vote of 148 to 2 the bill which banned Communist Party members from public office only to have it lost when the Senate failed to act after the Senate Civil Service Committee had substituted the Assembly measure for its own bill.

Another McMullen bill which prohibited the use of any public building by any group designated as subversive by the Attorney-General of the United States met with enthusiastic legislative approval and then succumbed to a veto by Governor Dewey.[7] Two additional attempts were made by Senator Scanlon to invoke legislative sanctions against Communist threats. On February 23, he introduced two bills, one to exclude from the ballot Communists and others advocating forcible overthrow of government, and the other to require an additional oath of all teachers in all educational institutions

[4] *New York Times,* February 23, 1949, p. 1.

[5] Assembly Int. 1694, No. 1757 (McMullen); Senate Int. 2112 (Scanlon), Feb. 10, 1949.

[6] Assembly Int. 1695, No. 1758 (McMullen); Senate Int. 2113 (Scanlon), Feb. 10, 1949.

[7] Assembly Int. 1693, No. 1756, February 10, 1949.

supported by state funds or whose real property is in whole or in part exempted from taxation.[8] The attempt to rule the Communist Party off the ballot was approved unanimously by the Senate; the Assembly was denied an opportunity to express its opinion when its Rules Committee killed the Senate bill.

The additional loyalty oath requirement for teachers, actually an amendment to the Ives Loyalty Oath Law of 1934, is particularly interesting because it illustrates the futility of this type of legislation. Finding the existing requirement an inadequate safeguard, the problem is met by demanding additional assurances from the untrustworthy profession. The language of the new provision is worth quoting:

> In addition to the foregoing oath [Ives Loyalty Oath], each such teacher, instructor and professor, within thirty days after the effective date of the amendment of this section hereby made, and each new teacher, instructor and professor before commencing upon his employment, shall make and file a sworn statement that he is not a member of, affiliated or associated with, any foreign or domestic organization, association, group, movement or combination of persons whose aims and principles are totalitarian, fascist, communist or subversive or who have adopted a policy advocating or approving the commission of acts of force or violence to deny other persons of their rights under the constitution of the United States, or seeking to alter the form of government of the United States by unconstitutional means.

The Provisions of the Feinberg Law

Instead of enacting the new loyalty oath bill, the legislature shifted its attention to the Feinberg bill introduced by the Senate Majority leader on March 11, 1949.[9] Section 3021 of Article 61 of the New York education law provides:

8 Senate Int. 2003, No. 2173; Senate Int. 2005, No. 2175.
9 Senate Int. 2624, Nos. 2977, 3101.

A person employed as superintendent of schools, teacher or employee in the public schools of the State shall be removed for the utterance of any treasonable or seditious word or words or the doing of any treasonable or seditious act or acts while holding such position.

The provision of the state education law must be considered in conjunction with Section 12-a of the New York civil service law (the Devany Law) which provides:

No person shall be employed in the service of the state nor as a superintendent, principal or teacher in a public school or state normal school or college or any other state educational institution who a) By word of mouth or writing wilfully and deliberately advocates, advises or teaches the doctrine that the government of the United States or any state or of any political subdivision thereof should be overthrown or overturned by force, violence or any unlawful means.

The Feinberg bill proposed to add a new Section 3022 to "eliminate subversive persons from the public school system." The new section, in effect, shifts legislative emphasis from substantive to procedural aspects of the loyalty program. It imposes upon the state educational authorities—the Board of Regents—the duty to enforce the law already on the books and stipulates in some detail the administrative procedures to be employed. Furthermore, by incorporating a requirement of annual detailed reports, the legislature virtually serves notice on the board that failure to produce tangible evidence of vigorous enforcement will invite trouble.

The second paragraph of the new section contains the procedural requirements:[10]

The board of regents shall, after inquiry, and after such notice and hearing as may be appropriate, make a listing of organizations which it finds to be subversive in that they advocate, advise,

[10] For the full text of the act see Appendix VII.

teach or embrace the doctrine that the government of the United States or of any state or of any political subdivision thereof shall be overthrown or overturned by force, violence or any unlawful means, or that they advocate, advise, teach or embrace the duty, necessity or propriety of adopting any such doctrine as set forth in Section twelve-a of the civil service law. Such listings may be amended and revised from time to time. The board, in making such inquiry, may utilize any similar listings or designations promulgated by any federal agency or authority authorized by federal law, regulation or executive order, and for the purposes of such inquiry, the board may request and receive from federal agencies or authorities any supporting material or evidence that may be made available to it. The board of regents shall provide in the rules and regulations required by subdivision one hereof that membership in any such organization included in such listing made by it shall constitute prima facie evidence of disqualification for appointment to or retention in any office or position in the public schools of the state.

Two features of the new proposal are worthy of particular notice. By indicating that the board of regents might make use of existing lists promulgated by federal agencies, the legislature in effect incorporated the Attorney-General's list of subversive organizations in its directive to the board. There is nothing to prevent the board from adding to the listings employed by the Attorney-General.

Once the list of proscribed organizations has been agreed upon, membership in any of these organizations shall be *prima facie* evidence of disqualification. In other words, even though an organization may be erroneously tabbed as subversive, once it is so designated its members are automatically stamped as subversive unless they can prove the contrary. Section 12d of the New York civil service law provides that in removal cases "the burden of sustaining the validity of the order of dismissal or ineligibility by a fair preponderance of the credible evidence shall be upon the person making such dismissal or order of ineligibility." Where alleged membership in subversive organizations is involved, however, the general rule of the civil service law is reversed. In a case involving that sort of allegation, the legislature apparently intends that the burden of proof shall rest upon the defendant rather than upon the person who ordered the removal.

Senator Feinberg's proposal elicited an immediate response. Among the groups who actively opposed the measure were the American Civil Liberties Union, the American Labor Party, the Citizens Union, the New York Chapter of the National Lawyers Guild, the New York State Council of the Arts, Sciences and Professions, the New York State CIO, the Public Education Association, the Teachers Union, Local 555, UPW-CIO, and the United Parents Association. Both the *New York Times* and the *Herald Tribune* took strong stands against the bill, and numerous public figures called upon the legislature to reject such dangerous legislation.

In striking contrast to the open and rather stridently vocal opposition voiced against the measure, those favoring it, represented chiefly by church, veteran, and patriotic groups, chose to carry on their work chiefly behind the scenes. The effectiveness of their support was amply demonstrated when the measure was approved by votes of 41 to 14 in the Senate and 122 to 25 in the Assembly.

Developments since the Enactment of the Feinberg Law

The period since the enactment of the Feinberg Law has witnessed many interesting developments. On April 22, the Board of Regents established a committee to devise means to put into effect the provisions of the Feinberg Law. The committee was directed to report its recommendations at the May meeting. In the meantime, several of the agencies which had originally opposed the passage of the bill now shifted their attack to the board; they united in a demand for public hearings on the merits of the act. At its May meeting the board rejected the request for hearings on the law itself on the ground that inasmuch as the law had been passed, a subordinate administrative agency had no choice but to carry out its provisions. Any hearings on the question of the law's validity could have no useful purpose.

The committee engaged in working out the procedures for enforcing the law encountered unforeseen obstacles, however, and was unable to report a plan to the board in May; so the matter was postponed until the June meeting. With the law scheduled to go into effect July 1, 1949, internal differences within the committee continued to thwart agreement. The June meeting of the board brought no action except a declaration that the list of subversive organizations would be announced on July 15. It now became clear that two different sets of problems divided board members. The first stumbling block centered upon the nature of the lists of subversive organizations to be promulgated. Literally thousands of letters from interested parties had poured in, and the board had not been able to agree upon a list. It was finally announced on July 1 that five of the organizations named were: the Communist Party of the United States, the Socialist Workers Party, the Workers Party, the Industrial Workers of the World, and the Nationalist Party of Puerto Rico.

The second issue dividing the committee involved the procedure for implementing the law itself. The chief points of difference centered on the desirability of a new loyalty oath and a questionnaire to elicit from teachers information on the organizations to which they belonged. Also in dispute was the machinery for trying teachers who were charged with membership in the outlawed organizations.

After the public hearings, at which not only the organizations summoned but also numerous other groups subjected the law to heavy attack, the long-awaited rules were issued. The chief points are summarized below:

1. The school authorities of each school district shall require one or more officials to report to them on each teacher each year, stating that there is or is not evidence that he has violated the statutory provisions referred to.
2. The school authorities shall dismiss charges or prefer formal charges within ninety days of receiving an adverse report.
3. If charges are preferred, the dismissal proceeding shall be those ordinarily employed.
4. The Board of Regents shall promulgate a list of subversive organizations.
5. Evidence of membership in any organization on the list ten days after its promulgation shall constitute *prima facie* evidence of disqualification.
6. Evidence of membership in an organization before it is listed shall be presumptive evidence that membership continues, in the absence of a showing that membership has been terminated "in good faith."
7. School authorities shall make annual reports to the Commissioner of Education; any persons found disqualified shall be reported immediately.

The rules just summarized were promulgated on July 15, but the oft-mentioned list of subversive organizations, the nucleus of the whole loyalty procedure, once more failed to materialize. The board announced that the list would now appear on September 16.

The Board of Regents has been subjected to widespread criticism from every side. Opponents of the Feinberg Law have attacked the board, first, for not providing open hearings on the merits of the law and, second, for attempting to put the law into operation. On the other side, those supporting the

law have criticized the board for its failure to act more posi-
tively and expeditiously.

The truth of the matter is that the board has been the victim
of circumstances over which it had no control. To enforce the
Feinberg Law so as to carry out the intent of the legislature
and at the same time to discharge its obligations as the top
policy-making body of the state educational system was difficult if not impossible. By the law the board was compelled to
take substantive actions and to establish procedures which in
the opinion of some members placed in jeopardy the traditional guarantees of academic freedom. Honest differences of
opinion within the board concerning the permissible limits
of restrictive action complicated the matter.

Following publication of the rules already mentioned, the
late State Commissioner of Education Francis T. Spaulding
issued a memorandum implementing the Regents' rules. This
memorandum, which was distributed to all school officials in
the state, included the following instructions:

The officials will face a twofold duty. It will be their responsibility to help the school authorities rid the school system of persons who "use their office or position to advocate and teach
subversive doctrines." On the other hand, it will be their responsibility so to conduct themselves and their inquiries as to
protect and reassure teachers who are not subversive.

The officials should bear in mind the fact that while statements
made in connection with an official charge of disloyalty are
legally privileged, no privilege attaches to gossip and the circu-
lation of rumor.

The writing of articles, the distribution of pamphlets, the
endorsement of speeches made or articles written or acts performed
by others, all may constitute subversive activity.

Nor need such activity be confined to the classroom. Treasonable or subversive acts or statements outside the school are as

much a basis for dismissal as are similar activities in school or in the presence of school children.

It must be borne in mind that teachers who are honestly concerned to help their pupils to become constructive citizens are likely to raise many questions and make many suggestions about possible improvements in the American form of government and American institutions, which cannot in any just sense be construed as subversive.

Moreover, teachers who take full advantage of their own privileges as citizens may raise questions and make suggestions outside their classrooms about improvements in our form of government. In addition, they may quite legitimately inform themselves fully, and enter into discussions with other people, about forms of government different from our own.

School authorities should reject hearsay statements, or irresponsible and uncorroborated statements, about what a teacher has said or done, either in school or outside. They should examine an accused teacher's statements, writing or action in their context, and not in isolated fragments. They must insist on evidence, and not mere opinion, as a basis for any action which they make take.

The Commissioner points out that under the law a teacher may be guilty of subversive activity if he writes articles or distributes pamphlets. He may also be engaged in subversive activity if he endorses speeches made, articles written, or acts performed by someone else. These actions need not occur in the classroom in order to render the teacher liable.

But while the memorandum is explicit in stating the several kinds of actions which may be subversive, no guidance is given concerning the nature of articles, speeches, or acts which would be regarded as objectionable.

The concluding sections of the memorandum introduce a note of caution by declaring that discussions of the American form of government and suggestions for its improvement may not be subversive, and officials are warned to reject hearsay or irresponsible, uncorroborated statements.

School officials charged with responsibility for administering the law as amplified by these instructions will hardly find here a sure guide for temperate enforcement. One can only suspect that the first part of the directive will receive greater emphasis than the latter.

The record of the State Commissioner of Education shows him to have been a person of judgment and tolerance. His attempt to implement a law that places such heavy premium upon conformity and yet to preserve an atmosphere favorable to academic freedom, although not reassuring, was probably the best that could be achieved.

The final chapters in the controversy can be sketched briefly. On September 12, 1949, preparatory to the law's going into effect on September 15, Superintendent of New York City Schools William Jansen issued instructions for administering the Feinberg Law and the Board of Regents' rules. The following day the Communist Party obtained a ten-day Supreme Court order restraining the Board of Regents from promulgating its list of subversive organizations. Within the next few days similar actions were taken by the Teachers Union and various citizens' groups. The initial restraining order was subsequently extended.

Late in November, 1949, in the first judicial test of the law on its merits, the Feinberg Law was declared unconstitutional. Justice Harry E. Schirick of the New York State Supreme Court, a court of first resort, ruled that the statute constituted a bill of attainder and that it contravened the due process clauses of the state and federal constitutions.

Justice Schirick defined a bill of attainder as "a legislative act which inflicts punishment without judicial trial," and pointed out that by the language of the Feinberg Law the Board of Regents was in effect directed to list the Communist Party as a subversive organization. His opinion continued:

199

The statute therefore violates the constitutional proscription of bills of attainder. It is a legislative finding of guilt of advocating the overthrow of government by unlawful means without a judicial trial and without any of the forms and guards provided for the security of the individual by our traditional judicial forms.

Justice Schirick found that the law transgressed the due process clause of the state and federal constitutions in four particulars: its vagueness, its procedures, its presumption of guilt, and its doctrine of guilt by association.

The State Attorney-General announced that an immediate appeal would be taken. In the meantime a separate challenge of the law resulted in a second Supreme Court decision on December 16, likewise ruling that the statute was unconstitutional because it violated the due process clauses of the state and federal constitutions and established guilt by association.

The victory of the anti-Feinberg group was short-lived, for on March 8, 1950, the Appellate Division, Third Department, reversed the decision of Justice Schirick and ruled unanimously in favor of the law. The court overruled the bill of attainder charge and concluded that the provisions of the law were not unreasonable infringements of teachers' rights. Three weeks later the second case was likewise overruled when on March 27 in another unanimous decision the Appellate Division, Second Department, reversed the decision that the Feinberg Law violated the due process clauses of the state and federal constitutions. Further appeal of both decisions was announced.

On November 30, 1950, the New York State Court of Appeals sustained the Feinberg Law.[11] Speaking for a unanimous court, Associate Judge Edmund H. Lewis observed that "when in its judgment and discretion the Legislature finds acts by public employees which threaten the integrity and compe-

[11] *Thompson v. Wallin,* 301, N.Y. 476.

tence of a governmental service such as the public school system, legislation adequate to maintain the usefulness of the service affected is necessary to forestall such danger. Believing the Feinberg Law to be the Legislature's answer to such a need we find in that statute no restriction which exceeds the Legislature's constitutional power."

Judge Lewis likened the Feinberg Law to a new strand in the mesh which the legislature had established to screen those selected to teach the state's children, and he called attention to such other strands as Section 2004 of the education law, which denies the right to serve as a teacher unless one has taken an oath to support the federal and state constitutions, and Section 801 of the same law, which requires school instruction in patriotism.

The opinion ruled that the Feinberg Law did not offend on the ground of due process. It was pointed out first that no organization could be listed by the Board of Regents as subversive until "after inquiry and after such notices and hearing as may be appropriate." On the much criticized provision that membership in any organization listed by the Board of Regents as subversive shall constitute prima-facie evidence of disqualification for appointment or retention, the court sustained the legislature but in so doing read into the law procedural interpretations which the bare words of the statute do not carry. Judge Lewis pointed out that under an earlier decision the presumption growing out of a prima-facie case remains only so long as there is no substantial evidence to the contrary. When such evidence is presented the presumption disappears and unless further proof is supplied there is nothing to justify a finding based solely on it.

In the language of the opinion, "thus the phrase prima facie evidence of disqualification as used in the statute *imports a hearing at which one who seeks appointment or retention in a public school position shall be afforded an opportunity to*

*present substantial evidence contrary to the presumption.
. . . Once such contrary evidence has been received . . . the
official who made the order of ineligibility has thereafter the
burden of sustaining the validity of that order by a fair preponderance of the evidence."* [12]

Judge Lewis added that if an order of ineligibility should be
issued against an individual, that person could avail himself
of the full procedural safeguards prescribed by the civil service
law.[13] He concluded: "Reading that statute [Feinberg Law]
in that way, as we do, we cannot say there is no rational relation
between the legislative findings which prompted the enactment of the Feinberg Law and the measures prescribed therein
to safeguard the public school system of the state."

This interpretation of the law has reduced although not
entirely removed some of its most dangerous features.

The Communist Party and the teachers' unions have declared their intention to carry the case to the United States
Supreme Court, but no decision has been rendered at this
writing.

[12] Italics added.   [13] See page 65, above.

VI

Conclusion

WHAT conclusions may be drawn from the foregoing account of a state legislature's efforts to deal with the threat of subversive activity during the past thirty years? Already, as occasion offered, opinions have been expressed on one or another aspect of the various legislative actions described. It seems appropriate to draw together in a fairly systematic manner some of the chief points which emerge from the study.

New York experience with legislative investigations of disloyalty, as represented by the Lusk, McNaboe, and Rapp-Coudert committees, presents a record of startling contrasts and disconcerting similarities. When examined against the background of the excesses and egregious nonsense of the Lusk and McNaboe investigations, the Rapp-Coudert inquiry seems exemplary, yet it must share with its more infamous predecessors the onus of smearing innocent people and of employing offensive procedures.

The Lusk committee violated almost every canon of responsible conduct. Neither the committee chairman nor his counsel and staff respected the customary limitations of orderly procedure. Not only did they as a common practice employ the tactics of the side-show barker and the old-time patent medicine hawker, they ranged recklessly over the entire area of individual rights with wanton disregard for such fundamentals as separation of powers or due process of law. It would be unreasonable to expect meritorious conduct or salutary results under these circumstances. The natural course would be to write off the Lusk investigation as a perversion and attribute its iniquities to this unfortunate happenstance. One does not appraise an institution or process upon the basis of the most degenerate sample.

Something of the same order of logic might be applied to the McNaboe investigation. Its brief chaotic existence was so marred by the ridiculous fulminations of the committee chairman that no one took it seriously enough for great harm to be done. Everyone recognized the highly personal nature of this particular exhibition and regarded it as disgraceful, but its excesses were not charged against the legislative investigation as an institution.

All the more disturbing, therefore, must be the reaction to the Rapp-Coudert committee. Here was an investigation tarnished by none of the hypocrisy or the buffoonery of its two predecessors. Those charged with its conduct were persons of integrity conscious of the responsibility under which they carried out their directive. All the evidence indicates that the Rapp-Coudert investigation was conducted by reasonable people with a high sense of personal honor and a keen desire to operate within the spirit of American democratic institutions. For these reasons it is particularly disquieting to face the fact that the record of the investigation reveals so many shortcomings. It proceeded from challengeable assumptions, employed procedures that produced unnecessary personal hardship and mental anxiety, and established precedents which weakened traditional principles of civil liberties and academic freedom.

The survey of New York experience suggests that whenever subversive activity becomes the subject of investigation by a politically constituted committee it is difficult to prevent in-

justices from occurring or innocent persons from being injured. One reason for this is the amorphous, undefinable
character of subversive activity. What to one group is subversive is to another merely criticism. Another reason is that
even granted that a particular act or course of action is subversive (destructive), it cannot be proscribed or rooted out
without doing serious injury to our traditional privilege of
free speech, which includes free criticism of existing governmental institutions and officials. Still another reason—one
particularly pertinent in the case of communism—is that
decision is derived by formula rather than based on tangible
factual evidence. Once the factor of communism enters the
picture, individuals *suspected of being Communists*—proof
is rarely established—are assumed to be invested with all the
qualities, objectives, and fanatical zeal of the most dedicated
party operative on record.

A committee set up to study subversive activity cannot resist the temptation to unearth "subversives." It naturally concentrates upon people—errant individuals and groups—and
its box score is determined by the number brought to book.
Unlike an investigation of factory conditions, or educational
expenditures, or milk prices, where the chief focus of attention
is upon the cause-and-effect factors of a particular area of our
business or social structure, the loyalty investigation concentrates upon the transgressor rather than upon the conditions
that have produced unrest. Police activities get all mixed up
with fact finding, to the detriment of the latter. In the case of
the Lusk investigation, what was supposed to be an investigation turned into a police activity with brazen disregard for
legal and ethical conventions.

No such charge is leveled against the Rapp-Coudert committee. Its conduct was at all times well within the canons of
legality; it indulged in none of the raids or searches and seizures
which were standard operating procedure for the Lusk com

mittee. Yet early in its work it accepted the view that its chief task was that of identifying Communists—a function smacking more of police work than of an investigating committee.

Some Suggested Procedural Safeguards

Some thoughtful observers have reached the conclusion that subversive activity is not a matter that can be profitably investigated by legislative committees. This view is based upon two grounds: additional legislation in this field is not appropriate or necessary; abuse of constitutional guarantees cannot be avoided. The record of the past is unequivocally clear on one point, however: legislative investigations *have* occurred. One can find nothing to indicate that they will not occur again.

Under these circumstances a more practical question arises: Can legislative investigations of subversive activities be adequately hedged in by procedural safeguards so as to prevent or at least minimize abuse? Before terminating this report some suggestions which have either grown out of or been reinforced by this study will be presented.

1. If a legislative committee is directed to look into the subject of subversive activity, the investigation should be limited to that single subject. Attention has already been called to the suspicion aroused because the Rapp-Coudert committee was directed to investigate school finances as well as subversive activities. Counsel Paul Windels acknowledged the error when he wrote in a letter to the *New York Times* that the two subjects should never have been joined and explained, "It was bound to subject the committee's inquiry into subversive activities to suspicion as to motives." [1]

For different but equally compelling reasons the McNaboe investigation gives added point to the single-purpose injunction. If the single-purpose principle had been observed, the

[1] *New York Times,* October 19, 1942, p. 18.

McNaboe investigation would never have occurred because the committee was established to investigate enforcement of the criminal law.

2. The investigation should be limited in scope, and the terms of reference of the committee should be carefully defined in the most specific language possible. This point is closely related to but distinct from number one. It becomes especially important when the inquiry falls into the hands of vindictive or irresponsible people. The Lusk committee roamed all over the law enforcement map without troubling to distinguish investigation from police administration.

Even in the case of the Rapp-Coudert committee, however, the omnibus character of the particular subsection of the resolution that applied exclusively to the Coudert subcommittee invited trouble. Subsection (i) authorized the subcommittee to look into "school administration," "methods and subject matter of instruction," "methods of appointment, removal and retirement," "the extent to which, if any, subversive activities may have been permitted," "practices and activities of the Municipal Civil Service Commission" in regard to positions under the supervision of the educational authorities. When the subcommittee concentrated on only one of these, it laid itself open to the charge that it was biased. Furthermore, the directive to determine "the extent to which" subversive activities exist gave it no framework within which to act. The committee's decision to concentrate upon the teachers' unions did not in all probability conform to what Senator Dunnigan had in mind when he introduced his resolution. The press comment at the time and, more important, the views expressed by educational authorities revealed a broader conception of the committee's work.

3. The investigation should be planned and conducted by a professional staff selected on the basis of the strictest specifi-

cations possible. If the investigation involves the schools, at least part of the staff and by all means the directing head should be a professional educator rather than a lawyer.

Lawyers have their place in investigations. By training and experience they are equipped to judge evidence and handle aspects of the investigation that impinge upon legal matters. But because of their training and background lawyers may emphasize the legal aspects of situations when their relevance is subordinate to other considerations. Furthermore, it is a curious paradox that it was the lawyers on the Coudert committee staff who insisted that because the hearings were not trials, the persons summoned were not entitled to the normal legal safeguards. Why then should it not follow with equal logic that lawyers were not the proper persons to conduct the hearing? Why not some person more fully familiar with the practices and methods of teachers and more sympathetic to the nuances or subtleties of academic activity? Certainly the lawyers did not make notable headway in eliciting the information they sought, despite the fact that they placed heavy reliance upon the customary legal devices—the subpoena, the oath and the cross-examination. Earlier reference has been made to the relatively greater results produced by the quiet research methods of the Rapp-Coudert committee after the work had been taken over by Dr. Strayer and his staff.

No attempt is made to suggest that the tasks of the Strayer group were as knotty and elusive as those which confronted the Coudert committee, but one wonders whether greater emphasis on methods other than trying to force reluctant participants to talk might not have produced more of the information sought. If, instead of trying to discover whether a particular individual had actually joined the Communist Party, the committee had focused its attention upon conditions in the schools and among members of the staff which produced low morale, insecurity, and resentment and had investigated factually to ascertain whether these teachers were engaged in activities actually destructive of democratic institutions, the investigation could never have taken the turn it did.

The committee staff constructed a hypothetical case and then sought evidence to substantiate this case. Had the investigators concentrated upon finding out just what the actual facts were instead of on marshaling evidence to support their case, their methods and their results might have been different.

Surely, if the underlying indictment against the accused teachers was that their party membership had poisoned their minds and destroyed their capacity to seek and teach the truth, then what could be more relevant than to search for evidence upon this point? Would not the classroom performance of suspected Communists be at least one test of their fitness as teachers? And certainly one valuable source of information upon this crucial question would be the persons who had taken courses from these teachers. Yet one searches vainly for evidence on this point or for any indication that serious attention was given to its relevance.

Possibly the committee was diffident about its ability to distinguish between appropriate and dangerous teaching. But what is the alternative? If a teacher's fitness to teach cannot be tested by what he does in his classroom, will greater justice and accuracy be achieved by basing its fitness upon such factors as the investigating committee stressed: his attendance at meetings, his marching in May Day parades, whether he read the *Daily Worker,* whether he collaborated in the publication and distribution of the *Teacher-Worker,* and so forth.

It seems likely that a staff of people familiar with academic methods and attitudes and employing techniques of research and fact finding would have produced more information useful to the legislature and to the general public than was adduced by the legalistic procedures employed by the Coudert subcommittee.

4. Any legislative investigation, but perhaps most of all an investigation of subversive activities, should pay more attention to its relationship to the general public. This is a controversial topic, and some observers believe that the only way to avoid the one extreme of abuse of publicity is to espouse the opposite extreme of no publicity. The difficulty of finding and pursuing some acceptable middle ground is not overlooked or minimized in this discussion. Indeed, the record of the three investigations here reported exemplifies vividly the alternative dangers. Both the Lusk and the McNaboe investigations provide examples of the damages that can be wrought by a publicity-seeking committee chairman or counsel. Innocent people are smeared and the government is discredited, while the underlying objective of the investigation—the elicitation of information—is lost in the shuffle. At almost the opposite extreme is the example of the Rapp-Coudert committee. Commendably reluctant to smear innocent people by the kind of reckless declarations which had characterized its predecessors, the committee also hesitated to explain its work to the public for less laudable reasons.

The Coudert committee erred by not attaching sufficient importance to the need for letting the general public know what it was doing. When the teachers' unions were so vehemently articulate in presenting the adverse side of the investigation, the public was entitled to a fair and full statement of the committee's side. The committee alone was in possession of the information necessary for setting forth this view. Whether it chose to do its own job of public information or whether it preferred that its side of the story should come from some other agency, the committee was responsible for seeing that this story was told. Because it did not gauge properly the importance of an informed public, the committee invited trouble in two ways.

Many liberal people who might have aided the committee

in making the investigation fruitful and worthwhile became alienated at the outset. Deprived of their counsel and co-operation, the committee pursued policies increasingly offensive to others and damaging to itself. This led the committee to conclude that it was misunderstood and unfairly censured by the very persons who should be supporting it. Obsessed with this conviction the committee decided that since it could not expect sympathetic support from the liberal element in the community, it was obliged to fight its battle alone. This attitude in turn induced an unconciliatory frame of mind on the part of the investigators and resulted in a more repressive and sometimes almost vindictive attitude. The incidents of the subpoenaing of teachers' union and students' union lists and the treatment of Charles J. Hendley seem to reflect something of this state of mind.

The experience of New York legislative committees strongly suggests that the problem of public information is central in investigations of subversive activities and that just as much harm can result from underemphasizing it as from its overemphasis or abuse. The task of the investigating committee is to recognize the importance of an adequately informed public and to take the steps necessary to make this possible. Unlike some aspects of the governmental process—for example, the apprehension of a criminal—the legislative investigation cannot be carried on in secrecy without going a long way toward defeating its purpose.

5. Provision should be made for the regularization of committee procedures to guarantee such elementary safeguards as may be required to protect the interests of persons concerned. Whether these procedural requirements should be made a part of the regular legislative law or whether they should be incorporated in the language of the authorizing resolution may be open to debate. In spite of the possible danger of making procedure unnecessarily rigid, some advantage lies

with the former because if the matter is left to the drafting committee, the necessary guarantees may disappear in the confusion that frequently accompanies the last-minute rush during which such resolutions sometimes assume their final form.

The scope which procedural guarantees should properly cover needs further study before a categorical proposal is advanced, but tentative suggestions may be presented. Investigating committees—whatever the subject under scrutiny—have usually tended to employ the customary apparatus of compulsory attendance and private inquisitorial procedures under oath, with considerable emphasis upon public testimony at some stage of the investigation. Much of the procedure resembles that which from time-honored custom has been an integral part of our court procedure—with three important exceptions. The individual under the spotlight in a legislative hearing is frequently not permitted: 1) presence of counsel; 2) confrontation by those who have testified against him with opportunity to cross-examine them; 3) examination of the written record of his interview or interrogation in order to ascertain that he has been correctly recorded.

The opinion has already been expressed that legislative investigative procedure has been unnecessarily legalized and that less formalized procedures would probably produce more useful information—the ostensible justification for having an investigation in the first place. So long as investigating committees insist upon employing the legal framework for their inquiry, however, they should go all the way rather than continue their present practice of taking over only part of the apparatus and omitting the rest. Two different sets of considerations dictate this assertion.

Only by extending to the person concerned the privileges enumerated above can the committee make sure that his interests will be protected—a minimum requirement for any governmental procedure if it is to be consonant with our constitutional system. The oft-reiterated argument is that an investigation is not a trial and that consequently the witness is not entitled to the guarantees extended to a person facing conviction on charges. Technically, a hearing and a trial are different, but from the standpoint of their effect upon the individual concerned it may well be that he may suffer greater injury from the hearing than from the trial. This brings us to the second reason why the committee should follow the principle of "all or none" in its adoption of trial procedures for conducting its hearings.

Only by according the witness full opportunity to cross-examine those who have made allegations concerning him and only by permitting him to correct the verbatim record in the event his testimony has been erroneously recorded can the committee gain the true facts that they are after. If the real purpose of the inquiry is to uncover information, the investigators can best achieve their objective by hearing both sides—not by contenting themselves with an *ex parte* view. If a judge or jury need to hear both sides—or, more specifically, if they need to have the testimony of any witness refined by exposing it to cross-examination by someone who views the issue or incident from a different vantage point—before arriving at a conclusion, should an investigating committee be willing to formulate its conclusion on less substantial bases? Only when all the facts are brought to light are the twin objectives of protection of the individual and enlightenment of the committee achieved.

6. Full and explicit provision should be made for the preservation of committee records. Existing practice on this point leaves much to be desired. A committee usually publishes a final report; in some instances one or more interim reports may also be issued. Frequently, however, the published reports of a committee fall far short of being adequate. The four massive volumes of the Lusk committee contain much ma-

terial only remotely related to the work actually performed by the committee, while the records of the hearings which the committee held in New York City and upstate were never made available. Somewhat the same comment can be made concerning the McNaboe and Rapp-Coudert committees. In the case of the McNaboe committee, because of the haphazard character of its operation its failure to preserve more fully its records is not of serious concern. The situation is different for the Coudert committee, however. In this instance the two preliminary reports and the final report embracing altogether approximately 530 pages are the only committee records readily available for examination. When one considers that the committee and its vigorous staff of six or more members functioned continuously for well over a year, this published record of its work is extremely meager. Actually, the committee amassed more than thirteen thousand pages of private testimony and about three thousand pages of public testimony; it also received almost six hundred exhibits in evidence. Added to this is the very considerable volume of supplementary material developed by the research staff.

Yet none of this material is accessible in any library or public depository where accredited persons can consult it. Except for the printed reports and the contemporary press accounts available in newspaper files, the chronicles of the important Coudert committee have all but evaporated within a decade of the investigation. What considerations have led to this situation and how has it come about?

On March 5, 1947, the Joint Committee on the State Educational System turned "all files of the subcommittee investigating education and subversive activities in the schools of New York City over to the Executive Department, Division of State Police." [2] It is not clear, however, just what has been

[2] State of New York, *Final Report of the Joint Legislative Committee on the Educational System,* Legislative Document (1947), No. 63, p. 88.

so transferred and what has not. Inquiry of the State Police reveals that the material has not yet been catalogued and that it is not open for inspection, even in response to legal process. Former members of the committee staff have indicated that the private hearings were not turned over to the State Police. It must, therefore, be assumed that they still remain in the possession of some of the committee or that they have been destroyed. There also seems to be doubt concerning the location of the exhibits. (Through the courtesy of the chairman of the subcommittee, the writer has been able to examine most of the testimony recorded during the public hearings. While this consideration is appreciated, one questions the desirability of an arrangement where access to such material must depend upon favor.)

The purpose of an investigation is to turn up information—primarily for the legislature but also and certainly ultimately for the general public. Legislatures are not supposed to function *in camera*. On what possible ground then can there be justification for withholding from the legislature and the public the facts uncovered by the investigation? Some may suggest that so long as the committee makes its report public its records are not needed. But the report is no substitute for the raw material of the hearings. Indeed, the hearings are an indispensable corrective to the report itself if one wishes to grasp fully the fruits and implications of the investigation.

Six points have been cited where procedural improvements seem desirable and feasible. A seventh item deserves mention before the subject is dismissed, although no specific recommendation is made. A point that occurs with conspicuous regularity is that investigating committees tend to make some of their most spectacular disclosures in the period immediately preceding the moment when their request for additional funds comes up. The pressure upon the committee to present a strong case for its continuance builds up to the danger point as the time for the crucial vote nears. At this time all forces counseling moderation, objective judgment, dispassionate fact finding are assailed by the chilling realization that no matter how fine a job the committee may have been doing in probing useful but unexciting dark spots, its likelihood of being extended is probably dependent upon its coming up with something hot.

Under such circumstances, the possibility of avoiding excessively inflammatory claims and extravagant promises is dangerously small. How can this temptation be avoided? An easy answer has not been found. It is well-nigh impossible and probably undesirable to force an investigating committee to complete its work in a single appropriating period. To permit the committee to continue to draw appropriations without some form of legislative review and reconsideration also has serious drawbacks. The problem is raised but no solution is suggested because none has been discovered.

Communism and the Schools

The experience of New York legislative investigations of subversive activity does not add much to an understanding of the problem of balancing security and freedom under twentieth-century conditions. Little has been done to illuminate the problem itself; less has been done to suggest positive therapeutic measures.

Inasmuch as neither the Rapp-Coudert committee nor its predecessors point the way toward meeting the problem posed by the presence of Communists among teaching staffs, the concluding remarks will deal with the broad problem itself rather than with some procedural aspect.

Many who accept without reservation the doctrine of a free intellectual market when applied to any other subject feel that in the case of communism the thesis must be revised. They take this view on the ground that intellectual integrity, the good which is to be preserved through the free-market formula, has already been destroyed in the case of a Communist, therefore he has nothing to contribute and nothing to protect because his mind is no longer free.

To the writer this argument is dangerous because it misses the main point and concentrates upon a minor issue. To argue that a Communist has already lost his freedom of choice and is, accordingly, unable to participate in the quest for truth is to state a thesis that may or may not be true depending upon the individual concerned. Certainly some Communists have freed their minds from the shackles of party dogma and dominance; experience offers proof that such a course of action is possible. It is not only a theoretical possibility; by the hard test of empirical evidence the claim stands up.

From a source which affords every reason to believe the facts are accurate the statement has been made that since 1919 more than one million persons have gone in and out of the Communist Party in the United States. The magnitude of this startling figure has been explained by the contradictory nature of two of the basic operating principles of the Communist Party in this country: heavy emphasis upon recruitment in order to obtain a mass organization; a parallel emphasis upon uncompromising acceptance of party discipline. In furtherance of the first objective, each local unit was always confronted with the necessity of meeting its assigned quota of new membership. As a consequence, the party could not afford to be too rigid in its eligibility requirements. On the other hand, political independence or deviation from the official party line handed down from above was not tolerated.

Under these circumstances a rapid turnover in party membership was to be expected, and the one million figure cited above becomes understandable. Such an unstable membership reduces sharply the force of the current argument that a person who joins the Communist Party has lost his freedom.

Apparently freedom is a more hardy plant than many people are willing to believe. At any rate a million ex-Communists in this country is heartening evidence to this effect.

If the channels in and out of the party are sufficiently open to permit the entry and exit of a million persons in the course of the past thirty years, the concept of party members' becoming prisoners intellectually, hence no longer free, needs serious qualification. The conclusion seems inescapable that if the number of ex-Communists in the United States far outweighs the number of active members, the traditional principle of the free market still provides the most effective instrument for counteracting communism. It should be emphasized that this statement is made solely with reference to the United States. Where the long arm of the secret police can snatch offending or apostate party members and condemn them to death or to the living death of a labor camp, the chances of a party member's ever regaining his intellectual freedom are small. No evidence has come to light that such conditions are operative in the United States, however. Instances of persons who have left the Communist Party without bodily harm or other punishment more serious than castigation in the party press are too well known to permit acceptance of the proposition that coercion is of major importance so far as Communist membership in the United States is concerned. One must conclude that American Communists are not beyond possible redemption.

So long as there remains some uncertainty as to the futility of the free-market formula, so long as it may work in some cases, even though it is likely to fail in others, and so long as acute considerations of military security cannot be cited as justification for its suspension in favor of more extreme remedies, the arguments for its application to Communists seem just as strong as for any other dissident group.

There is something particularly offensive in the idea of permitting Communists to use the schoolroom as a vantage point from which to poison the minds of innocent and unsuspecting children. Anyone who would so prostitute the principles of the teaching profession as to use his classroom for proselytizing his students has undoubtedly forfeited the right to claim any constitutional protection on his own behalf. But there is a danger that by concentrating too sharply upon the offending teacher one loses sight of the deeper issue. Certain assumptions need to be clarified.

In the first place, the general acceptance of the effectiveness of the indoctrinating Communist teacher calls for further examination than it has yet received. Surprisingly little factual information has been assembled to document the general assumption that a Communist teacher can actually convert his students to communism. It is not the intention here to argue the point one way or the other, but the fact remains that our information on this question is far too meager to provide an adequate basis for judgment. Until we possess more factual data to test the popular assumption that Communist teachers are actually as dangerous as they are supposed to be, it can be argued that this assumption has been overplayed. In the absence of the information needed, one can offer certain a priori reasons for questioning the validity of the assumptions usually taken for granted. How often does a single teacher make such a deep impact upon his students that his views become a controlling influence on their minds? Under modern city school conditions—and it is reasonable to assume that Communist teachers would operate there rather than in the rural areas— no single teacher has uncontested monopoly over the students' minds. He is one of several persons from whom the student receives instruction. What he says and does must compete with the words and actions of several other teachers, presumably as able, articulate, and persuasive as he. Furthermore, the student spends more time outside the classroom than within. He is exposed to the views, prejudices, and wisdom of his own family, that of his friends and their parents, and that of the host of extra-school contacts that he develops.

Information is lacking from which the counteractive influence of these diverse contacts can be weighed, but until it is available, there is no reason to believe the student is completely impotent against the Communist teacher. The possibility of indoctrinating students with subversive ideas by an infected teacher under modern American conditions is flattering to the teaching profession, but I doubt that it will bear close scrutiny. In an era when the comic strip, the movie melodrama, and the radio thriller have demonstrably greater influence upon the interests and values of the younger generation than the individual schoolteacher, more tangible evidence of actual subversion should be produced before allegedly Communist teachers are fired on general principle without more persuasive proof of their destructiveness.

This leads to another aspect of this problem—one that renders even more complicated the doctrine that Communist teachers should be liquidated. How does one identify a Communist? What problems does the question of identification raise? What price can be considered reasonable for purging Communists? How many non-Communists should also be purged because they cannot prove beyond peradventure of doubt that they are not Communists? If one subscribes to the thesis that Communists per se are dangerous, then anyone who acts enough like a Communist to fall under suspicion—of the most suspicious person—must also be removed in order to be on the safe side. Where does it end?

These questions may appear to be a *reductio ad absurdum,* but such is not the case. Certainly the experience of the Rapp-Coudert investigation—the most reasonable and well-conducted inquiry of its kind that has come to my attention—does not suggest that the fact of party membership can easily be established. The evidence presented by the committee and later by the education authorities was circumstantial and contradictory in many cases. To the outsider the evidence assembled does not establish the fact of party membership beyond that reasonable doubt which honored custom decrees must be met before a person is adjudged guilty. In the single instance when a third agency was called upon to review the trial record he did not find the evidence sufficiently convincing to sustain the finding of the Board of Higher Education. Proof in these cases is elusive.

All of this should raise serious doubts as to the efficacy of a procedure which depends for its usefulness upon verification that frequently cannot be obtained. The administering authority must either permit some Communists to continue in employment (because incontrovertible proof cannot be adduced), thus defeating the purpose of the rule, or it must wield its axe freely and cut adrift all who *may be* Communists because they cannot *prove* their innocence. In the latter instance not only are innocent persons injured but all teachers are put on notice that the only course of action open if they wish to retain their jobs is to play it safe, to become routineers, yes men, Caspar Milquetoasts.

If there is anything that can make our schools dangerous threats to democracy it is a policy which attracts as teachers only those among our population who have neither the intellectual vigor nor the imagination to ask questions, to criticize, to offer suggestions. Democracy is posited upon the possibility and desirability of change. Change can mean progress only if it is purposive, selective. How can the generations which follow meet the challenge of a dynamic world if they receive their classroom instruction from a staff from which all vitality has been removed?

Appendix I

*Concurrent Resolution Authorizing the Investigation of
Seditious Activities
March, 1919*

WHEREAS, It is a matter of public knowledge that there is a large number of persons within the State of New York engaged in circulating propaganda calculated to set in motion forces to overthrow the Government of the State and the United States, and

Whereas, Sufficient facts were adduced by the sub-committee of the Senate of the United States investigating this subject during the last session of Congress to indicate the necessity of further inquiry and action, and

Whereas, It is the duty of the Legislature of the State of New York to learn the whole truth regarding these seditious activities and to pass when such truth is ascertained such legislation as may be necessary to protect the government of the State and to insure the maintenance of the rights of its citizens,

Now, Therefore, Be It Resolved, That a joint committee of the Senate and Assembly be, and hereby is, created to consist of four members of the Senate to be appointed by the Temporary President of the Senate, and five members of the Assembly, to be appointed by the Speaker of the Assembly, of which joint committee the Temporary President of the Senate and the Speaker of the

Assembly shall be members ex-officio, to investigate the scope, tendencies, and ramifications of such seditious activities and to report the result of its investigation to the Legislature; and be it

Further Resolved, That the said special committee shall have power to select its chairman and other officers to compel the attendance of witnesses and the production of books and papers; to employ counsel, stenographers and necessary clerical assistance; and shall have power to sit anywhere within the State, and shall otherwise have all the power of a legislative committee as provided by the Legislative Law, including the adoption of rules for the conduct of its proceedings, and be it

Further Resolved, That the sum of thirty thousand dollars ($30,000), or so much thereof as may be necessary, be and hereby is appropriated from the funds set aside for the contingent expenses of the Legislature, to be paid by the Treasurer on warrants of the Comptroller upon the certificates of the Chairman of the Committee and the approval of the Temporary President of the Senate or the Speaker of the Assembly. (*Report of the Joint Legislative Committee of the State of New York Investigating Seditious Activities*, 1920.)

Appendix II

The McNaboe Resolution
May 13, 1936

WHEREAS, National security and the future well being of our citizens and institutions are being jeopardized by skillfully organized and directed propaganda, and

Whereas, Leaders in this subversive and un-American activity have moved to poison the minds of students in our high schools and colleges with disloyal doctrines, thereby enlisting their support of movements and organizations known to be entirely alien to American ideals and traditions, and

Whereas, Our students are daily exposed to seditious or treasonable utterances in literature openly circulated in school rooms, assembly halls, on the campus and in school official publications, as well as from the lips of faculty members, and

Whereas, Professional paid agitators and propagandists are intimidating students in order to force their alliance with a so-called "United Front" that purposes to overthrow our Constitutional form of government and establish "a new social order," said end to be gained through revolutionary tactics, admittedly illegal and unconstitutional, and

Whereas, Faculty members have engendered factional strife among students by either taking the part of radical groups or else stifling patriotic acts of loyal students, and

Whereas, Known radicals are not only permitted to address students and advocate sabotage and disloyal acts, but are invited to do so by faculty members, and

Whereas, In our high schools and colleges, radical un-American groups, notably Communists, cause to be published and distributed among students and faculty members literature which advocates the overthrow of our present form of government and the setting up of a new social order, and further offers veiled threats against students and faculty members who do not join the revolutionary group, and

Whereas, the R.O.T.C. Units in some of our schools have been subjected to persecution, ridicule and sometimes been actually hampered in their efforts to equip themselves as loyal citizens and capable factors in our National Defense, and

Whereas, Disloyal faculty members and equally disloyal students have in many schools, because of their un-American activities and subversive campaigns, brought about demoralization of student groups, to the end that the students have been unable to efficiently carry on their studies and reap the rich benefits to which they are entitled, as free Americans, under our Constitution, and

Whereas, School facilities have been used as meeting places for parents and students, where un-American doctrines have been taught, and this with the knowledge and consent, as in the case of New York City, of the board of education, and

Whereas, Students on state scholarships, paid for by the taxpayers of the State of New York, openly advocate the overthrow of the United States government and the establishment of a Soviet America, with Moscow as the new seat of government, and

Whereas, Approximately 200 [sic] students from New York City, representing schools supported wholly or in part by State funds, recently went as official delegates to Columbus, Ohio, and by their votes aided in forming the American Students' Union, and endorsed its principles which pledge its members to work for the overthrow of the United States government, the setting up of a new social order, and

226

Whereas, This American Students' Union includes in its platform that its members pledge to support their government in no war it may be involved in but leaves them free to defend the Soviet Union, and

Whereas, The said students' union is pledged to seek the abolition of the R.O.T.C., [*sic*] the disarmament of the United States, which would reduce the nation to a state of unpreparedness and helplessness in an emergency, and

Whereas, The said union came into being through the machinations, not of bona fide students, and is officered by non-students, and

Whereas, Said organizers of the union and officers thereof are members of or agents of groups having international affiliations as well as being disloyal in acts and teachings, and

Whereas, Public moneys of the State of New York are invested in and contribute to the maintenance of public schools and colleges affected by these indictments, therefore be it

Resolved (if the Assembly concur) that a joint legislative committee be and it is hereby created, to consist of three Senators, to be appointed by the Temporary President, and three members of the Assembly, to be appointed by the Speaker of the Assembly, to make a complete and thorough investigation into the above-mentioned abuses. Said committee may sit and conduct its investigations within or without the State; take and hear proofs and testimony; subpoena and compel the attendance of witnesses, the production of books, records and documents; employ counsel, clerks, assistants and such other employees, needed by the committee properly to perform its functions hereunder and to fix the compensation of each within the amounts appropriated therefor; that such committee shall have all such further powers as are conferred upon legislative committees generally by the Legislative Law, and be it further

Resolved (if the Assembly concur) that such committee report to the Legislature on or before the first day of February, nineteen hundred and thirty-seven, and there be and there is hereby appropriated from the contingent fund of the Legislature for the expenses actually and necessarily incurred by said committee the sum of one hundred and fifty thousand dollars ($150,000), or so much thereof as may be necessary, payable on the audit and warrant of the Comptroller in the manner approved by law. (*New York Senate Journal,* 159th Session, 1936, I, 50–53.)

Appendix III

Recommendations of the McNaboe Committee

SOME recommendations concerning Nazism and Fascism are contained in that part of the report dealing with those subjects. The committee recommends that legislation be passed as soon as possible to outlaw the Communist Party. Such legislation should be drafted so as to cover the presently "camouflaged" activities of the Reds.

It should be made unlawful for any person who occupies the position of professor or teacher in the schools or universities of the State to advocate, defend, or propagate orally or in writing the doctrines of Communism.

No member of the Communist Party should be permitted to fill a State or local government position.

Membership lists of all political associations, parties, organizations and fronts should be filed annually with a duly authorized State authority.

It should be made unlawful for any person or persons to maintain, finance or organize "popular fronts" for the Communist cause.

No literature should be permitted to be printed, sold, displayed or distributed for the purpose of spreading the doctrines of Communism.

No money should be permitted to be collected, donated, or

solicited for foreign "isms" to be spent either here or in a foreign country.

Legislation should outlaw any attempts to control trade unions for the spread of foreign doctrines and propaganda.

The committee is of the opinion that the vast scope of the Communist activities justifies further investigation. There is no doubt in the minds of the members of this committee that startling disclosures can be made if the study of the problem is continued. Time and other factors have necessarily limited this investigation but the dangerous state of affairs already existing and not merely probable can and must be remedied.

The committee recommends that legislation be passed similar in form to the following:

"No society, association or corporation which, as a part of its constitution, by-laws, ritual or regulations, requires its members to take an oath or obligation in conflict with or repugnant to the provisions of the Constitution of the State of New York, or the Constitution of the United States, or requires its members to hold their allegiance to some other government, power, person or influence, shall be organized or permitted to exist or function within the State of New York, and no person who belongs to any such society, association or corporation, and who owes allegiance to any government, king, potentate, power or person other than the government of the United States, shall be inducted into or hold a public office within the State of New York. Any society, association, corporation or individual, violating any of the provisions of this section shall be subject to a fine of not less than one thousand ($1,000) dollars nor more than five thousand ($5,000) dollars.

"Any person in this State, who shall carry or cause to be carried, or publicly display any red flag or other emblem or banner, indicating disloyalty to the government of the United States or a belief in anarchy or other political doctrines or beliefs whose objects are either the disruption or destruction of organized government, or the defiance of the laws of the United States or of the State of New York, shall be deemed guilty of a felony, and upon conviction shall be punished by imprisonment in the penitentiary of the

State of New York for a term not exceeding ten (10) years, or by a fine not exceeding one thousand dollars ($1,000), or by both such imprisonment and fine.

"Section 1. Chapter fifteen of the laws of nineteen hundred nine, entitled 'An act in relation to the civil service of the State of New York and the civil divisions and cities thereof, constituting chapter seven of the consolidated laws,' is hereby amended by adding three new sections, to be sections twelve-a, twelve-b and twelve-c, respectively, to read as follows:

"12-a. Ineligibility. No person shall occupy any office or position in the classified service of the state or of any civil division or city thereof for which civil service rights shall be established pursuant to this chapter, nor shall any persons be employed in the public service as superintendents, principals or teachers in a public school or academy or in a state normal school or college, or any other state educational institute who—

"(a) By word of mouth or writing advocates, advises or teaches the duty, necessity or propriety of overthrowing or overturning organized government by force or violence, or by assassination of the executive head or of any of the executive officials of government, or by any unlawful means; or,

"(b) Prints, publishes, edits, issues or knowingly circulates, sells, distributes or publicly displays any book, paper, document, or written or printed matter in any form, containing or advocating, advising or teaching the doctrine that organized government should be overthrown by force, violence or any unlawful means; or,

"(c) Openly, wilfully and deliberately justifies by word of mouth or writing the assassination or unlawful killing or assaulting of any executive or other officer of the United States or of any state or of any civilized nation having an organized government because of his official character, or any other crime, with intent to teach, spread or advocate the propriety of the doctrines of criminal anarchy or communism as defined hereinafter; or,

" (d) Organizes or helps to organize or becomes a member of or voluntarily assembles with any society, group or assembly of persons formed to teach or advocate the propriety of the doctrines of criminal anarchy or communism as defined hereinafter.

"12-b. Criminal anarchy defined. Criminal anarchy is the doctrine that organized government shall be overthrown by force or violence, or by assassination of the executive head or of any of the executive officials of government, or by any unlawful means.

"12-c. Communism defined. Communism is the doctrine which advocates the destruction of the state by force and violence and the establishment of the dictatorship of the proletariat or which advocates the suppression of freedom of speech.

"2. This act shall take effect immediately."

The committee calls upon the American press, that great disseminator of truth, to conduct an active campaign against communism and expose the "fellow travellers."

The people of this country have secured the freedom of our press by the state and Federal constitutions.

That right as well as other inalienable rights, is now threatened by an international party controlled by Moscow, but our American press can destroy Communism overnight by particularly exposing the "fellow travellers."

The committee therefore requests the co-operation of the press in promoting the cause of Americanism, the enlightenment of our people, and our common welfare as a Nation.

It is also suggested that a resolution memorializing the Federal Congress be passed by both houses of our State Legislature in form as follows:

"Whereas, The report of the Joint Legislative Committee to investigate the Administration and Enforcement of Law establishes that a serious and dangerous situation exists within the State of New York by reason of the organizations and propaganda fostered by foreign governments whose basic philosophies of government are inimicable [sic] to that of our own American form of government; and

"Whereas, New York is the point of emanation of this foreign propaganda which threatens to render conditions as serious throughout the Nation as they now are in this State; and

"Whereas, The danger aforementioned has been brought about by the activities in this country of the disciples of Communism, Nazism and Fascism assisted by their European breeding grounds, Russia, Germany and Italy; and

"Whereas, Our forefathers, suffering under the economic and religious oppression and tyrannies of Europe over two centuries ago, founded upon these shores a government of the people and intended for the security and protection of natural liberties; and

"Whereas, Those oppressed peoples searching for life, liberty and happiness convened and drafted, as the basic and structural law of this land exemplifying their ideals, a Constitution of the people guaranteeing freedom of religion, freedom of speech, freedom of the press and the right of peaceful assembly; and

"Whereas, This Nation has thrived and prospered on the principles of true freedom and liberty secured to all as inalienable rights by that Constitution; and

"Whereas, Certain European nations have returned to that oppressive form of government which caused our forefathers in their wisdom to found this Nation; and

"Whereas, The efforts of these European agents are wholly un-American and violative of the constitutional guarantees because they abuse the rights secured by our government in order to totally destroy them; and

"Whereas, These emissaries are unwilling to test their theories by fair methods upon the American mind but instead bore from within our government, labor unions, churches, army, navy, educational institutions, hospitals, relief bureaus, unemployment insurance departments and civil service and elsewhere until such time as they are strong enough to control us and to employ force and violence; now, therefore be it

"*Resolved* (if the Assembly concur), That the Congress of the United States be and it is hereby memorialized to take such action by legislative enactment as will protect citizens of the United States in the security of their inalienable rights against those foreign emissaries (alien or citizen) who stand guilty of crimes against our Constitution; and be it

"*Further Resolved,* That the Congress of the United States be and it is hereby memorialized to investigate the source of finances used in promoting propaganda, and to adopt appropriate legislation to deal with the dissemination of foreign propaganda." (*New York Legislative Documents,* 162nd Session, 1939, XXIII, No. 98, 279–282.)

Appendix IV

Dunnigan Resolution
March 22, 1940

WHEREAS, attention has been drawn to the inference that the growth of the un-American and subversive organizations among the youth in attendance at the public schools and colleges of the City of New York is the result of the sponsorship and encouragement by the present administration of the New York City School System by resolutions and by-laws which authorize and encourage the formation and development of these organizations at will.

Whereas, it is charged that teachers and educational officials are members of organizations propagating the un-American theories of these organizations, that the facilities of the buildings in the various institutions have been extended to groups teaching class and racial hatreds, that indecent and immoral literature and school periodicals are openly distributed in the various schools and colleges, and that shocking and immoral conditions exist in the high schools and colleges.

Whereas, it has been alleged officials presently in charge of the administration of these institutions have persistently ignored the appeals and protests of parents and taxpayers and insist on conducting them in accordance with their own particular code of morals and their so-called liberal theories and philosophies, ignoring the fact that they are acting in a representative capacity on behalf of the taxpayers of the city and state who support their schools and colleges and who have a right to demand that the ideals and principles of every citizen, whether Catholic, Protestant, or Jew, shall at all times be respected, and that no political or pedagogical influence shall be injected to interfere with the inalienable rights guaranteed to our citizens.

Whereas, the many causes for complaint and indignation as hereinabove set forth clearly indicate the necessity of a thorough legislative investigation of the public educational system, of the City of New York, including the alleged subversive practices in such system, which it is charged have been condoned, if not actually encouraged by the Board of Education and the Board of Higher Education and including the coercive methods of such boards in intimidating educators in such system to the point where their usefulness may be seriously impaired, if, in fact, they are not forced to withdraw from educational work.

Now, therefore, be it resolved (if the Assembly concur), that a joint legislative committee be and is hereby constituted to consist of 5 members of the Senate to be appointed by the Temporary President of the Senate and 5 members of the Assembly to be appointed by the Speaker of the Assembly, with full power to investigate, inquire into, and examine the administration and conduct of the public educational system of the City of New York, including the Board of Education and the Board of Higher Education;

To make a thorough study and investigation of any and all persons and method of appointment of such persons holding positions in the supervisory, teaching, custodian and administrative staffs;

To carefully inquire into the extent to which subversive activities have been permitted to be carried on in the schools and colleges of such public school system; the extent to which the legal obligation to teach patriotic and proper civic training has been ignored;

To investigate any abuses of academic freedom in which coercive methods have been used to force the resignations of outstanding educators in the colleges of higher learning;

To inquire into the practices and activities of the Municipal Civil Service Commission in conducting examinations, promulgating lists, and certifying appointments to positions under the supervision of said Board of Education and Board of Higher Education. (*New York State Senate Journal,* 163rd Session, 1940, I, 323.)

Appendix V

Joint Resolution
March 29, 1940

WHEREAS, the Constitution of the State of New York mandates the legislature to "provide for the maintenance and support of a system of free common schools, wherein all children of this state may be educated," and

Whereas, many of the laws enacted by the legislature to carry out such mandate have become obsolete, and

Whereas, changes in social and economic conditions affecting educational needs, their support and maintenance, have occurred and are occurring, and

Whereas, the use of money appropriated by the state for our public schools has become the subject of widespread comment and public discussion, and

Whereas, the raising and appropriation of huge sums of public moneys for the maintenance and support of an ever-expanding educational system and the construction and equipment of new schools and appurtenances under existing laws have created a heavy burden of taxation, now, therefore, be it

Resolved (if the Senate concur), 1. That a joint legislative committee be and hereby is created and empowered to investigate, review and study (a) the procedure and methods employed to allocate state moneys for school and other educational purposes and the expenditure of the moneys so allocated for such purposes as prescribed by statute; (b) variations which should be made in the formulae by which such moneys are allocated and apportioned to localities for the support and aid of common schools and other statutory educational purposes due to the increased cost of educational activities; (c) additional educational facilities which are necessary and the formulae on the basis of which state moneys for such facilities might be apportioned; (d) the financial ability of the state to support education, particularly in relation to the co-ordination of state and local tax systems; (e) the methods by which school districts are laid out in the state and the effect of the present school district frame work upon the equalization of educational opportunity and upon the need for state aid; (f) the comparative needs of an educational system situated in intensively populated urban centers in contradistinction to communities in less populated areas; (g) the manner in which plans and specifications for the construction of school buildings are prepared and approved, including the nature of the requirements thereof and of the work performed thereunder; (h) the maintenance and administration of public schools and all other educational facilities; (i) the administration and conduct of the public school system of the City of New York, including the Board of Education and the Board of Higher Education; methods and subject matter of instruction; methods of appointments, removal and retirement of persons holding positions in the supervising, teaching, custodian and administrative staffs; the extent to which, if any, subversive activities may have been permitted to be carried on in the schools and colleges of such educational system; the practices and activities of the Municipal Civil Service Commission in the conduct of examinations, promulgation of lists and certification of appointments to positions under the supervision of the said Board of Education and Board of Higher Education; and (j) every other matter or thing not specifically set forth herein which may be deemed by such committee to be relevant to the general subject of its study, inquiry or investigation as though the same had been expressly set forth herein.

2. That such committee shall consist of six members appointed by the temporary president of the Senate, four of whom shall be Senators and the other two may but need not be Senators, and seven members appointed by the speaker of the Assembly, five of whom shall be members of the Assembly and the other two may but need not be members of the Assembly.

3. That such committee is authorized to choose a chairman and vice-chairman from its members to adopt rules for the conduct of its proceedings, to employ a secretary, counsel, investigators and such other assistants and employees as it may deem necessary.

4. That the members of such committee shall receive no compensation for their services, but shall be entitled to their necessary expenses and disbursements incurred by them in the discharge of their duties.

5. That such committee shall have power to fix the compensation of its secretary, counsel, investigators and other assistants and employees and to engage a suitable office or offices for the conduct of its investigations.

6. That such committee is authorized to sit in one or more parts at any place within the state and hold either public or private hearings.

7. That such committee and each member thereof shall have power to administer oaths, take testimony, subpoena and compel the attendance of witnesses and the production of all books, papers, records or documents deemed material or pertinent to its work, and shall generally have, possess and exercise all of the powers of a legislative committee as provided by the legislative law.

8. That such committee may request and shall receive from the department of education of the state, the board of education of any city or school district and from any other department, division, board, bureau, commission or agency of the state, or of any civil division thereof, such assistance and data as will enable it properly to complete its work hereunder.

9. That such committee shall report to the legislature with all convenient speed the result of its investigations with any legisla-

tive proposals which it recommends, and shall make its final report on or before February first, nineteen hundred forty-one.

10. That the sum of thirty thousand dollars ($30,000), or so much thereof as may be necessary, be and hereby is appropriated from the contingent fund of the legislature for the necessary expenses of such committee, to be paid from the treasury on audit and warrant of the comptroller upon vouchers of the chairman of such committee, approved and audited according to law. (*Report of the Subcommittee of the Joint Legislative Committee to Investigate Procedures and Methods of Allocating State Moneys for Public School Purposes and Subversive Activities,* Legislative Document [1942], No. 49.)

Appendix VI

Joint Resolution
January 8, 1941

WHEREAS, the Senate and Assembly of the State of New York, on March 29, 1940, adopted a concurrent resolution reading as follows:

Whereas, the Constitution of the State of New York mandates the legislature to "provide for the maintenance and support of a system of free common schools, wherein all children of this state may be educated," and

Whereas, many of the laws enacted by the legislature to carry out such mandate have become obsolete, and

Whereas, changes in social and economic conditions affecting educational needs, their support and maintenance, have occurred and are occurring, and

Whereas, the use of money appropriated by the state for our public schools has become the subject of wide-spread comment and public discussion, and

Whereas, the raising and appropriation of huge sums of public moneys for the maintenance and support of an ever-expanding educational system and the construction and equipment of new schools and appurtenances under existing laws have created a heavy burden of taxation, now, therefore, be it

Resolved (if the Assembly concur), 1. That a joint legislative committee be and hereby is created and empowered to investigate, review and study (a) the procedure and methods employed to allocate state moneys for school and other educational purposes and the expenditure of the moneys so allocated for such purposes as prescribed by statute; (b) variations which should be made in the formulae by which such moneys are allocated and apportioned to localities for the support and aid of common schools and other statutory educational purposes due to the increased cost of educational activities; (c) additional educational facilities which are necessary and the formulae on the basis of which state moneys for such facilities might be apportioned; (d) the financial ability of the state to support education, particularly in relation to the co-ordination of state and local tax systems; (e) the methods by which school districts are laid out in the state and the effect of the present school district frame work upon the equalization of educational opportunity and upon the need for state aid; (f) the comparative needs of an educational system situated in intensively populated urban centers in contra-distinction [sic] to communities in less populated areas; (g) the manner in which plans and specifications for the construction of school buildings are prepared and approved, including the nature of the requirements thereof and of the work performed thereunder; (h) the maintenance and administration of public schools and all other educational facilities; (i) the administration and conduct of the public school system of the City of New York, including the Board of Education and the Board of Higher Education; methods and subject matter of instruction; methods of appointments, removal and retirement of persons holding positions in the supervising, teaching, custodian and administrative staffs; the extent to which, if any, subversive activities may have been permitted to be carried on in the schools and colleges of such educational system; the practices and activities of the Municipal Civil Service Commission in the conduct of examinations, promulgation of lists and certification of appointments to positions under the supervision of the said Board of Education and

243

Board of Higher Education; and (j) every other matter or thing not specifically set forth herein which may be deemed by such committee to be relevant to the general subject of its study, inquiry or investigation as though the same had been expressly set forth herein.

2. That such committee shall consist of six members appointed by the temporary president of the Senate, four of whom shall be Senators and the other two may but need not be Senators, and seven members appointed by the speaker of the Assembly, five of whom shall be members of the Assembly and the other two may but need not be members of the Assembly.

3. That such committee is authorized to choose a chairman and vice-chairman from its members, to adopt rules for the conduct of its proceedings, to employ a secretary, counsel, investigators and such other assistants and employees as it may deem necessary.

4. That the members of such committee shall receive no compensation for their services, but shall be entitled to their necessary expenses and disbursements incurred by them in the discharge of their duties.

5. That such committee shall have power to fix the compensation of its secretary, counsel, investigators and other assistants and employees and to engage a suitable office or offices for the conduct of its investigation.

6. That such committee is authorized to sit in one or more parts at any place within the state and hold either public or private hearings.

7. That such committee and each member thereof shall have power to administer oaths, take testimony, subpoena and compel the attendance of witnesses and the production of all books, papers, records or documents deemed material or pertinent to its work, and shall generally have, possess and exercise all of the powers of a legislative committee as provided by the legislative law.

8. That such committee may request and shall receive from the department of education of the state, the board of educa-

tion of any city or school district and from any other department, division, board, bureau, commission or agency of the state, or of any civil division thereof, such assistance and data as will enable it properly to complete its work hereunder.

9. That such committee shall report to the legislature with all convenient speed the result of its investigations with any legislative proposals which it recommends, and shall make its final report on or before February first, nineteen hundred forty-one.

10. That the sum of thirty thousand dollars ($30,000), or so much thereof as may be necessary, be and hereby is appropriated from the contingent fund of the legislature for the necessary expenses of such committee, to be paid from the treasury on audit and warrant of the comptroller upon vouchers of the chairman of such committtee, approved and audited according to law.

Whereas, such committee was thereafter duly created and has commenced its investigation, review and study of the matters and things referred to it by the terms of said resolution, and

Whereas, it now appears that said Committee has not completed its investigation, review and study of the matters and things referred to it by the terms of said resolution, and will be unable to do so on or before February 1, 1941, and

Whereas, it is the judgment of this body that said Committee should be continued for another year for the effectuation of the purposes set forth in said resolution, and

Whereas, the right of said Committee to obtain certain necessary and pertinent evidence and effectively to inform itself through the medium of private hearings held before a single member has been questioned by numerous witnesses subpoenaed to attend and give testimony pursuant to the terms and provisions of such resolution, with the result that the work of said Committee has been delayed, and

Whereas, in the judgment of this body, the provisions of said resolution, whereby it was intended to confer upon said Committee the power effectively to conduct its investigation through the medium of hearings held in public or private before any member of said Committee sitting as a sub-committee of one, should be clarified and made more explicit,

Now, Therefore, Be It

Resolved (if the Assembly concur), that said Joint Legislative Committee be, and the same hereby is, continued with each and every of the powers expressly or impliedly given it by the provisions of said resolution, including the power thereby vested in each member of such Committee acting as such and as a sub-committee of one, to administer oaths, take testimony, subpoena and compel the attendance of witnesses and the production of all books, papers, records or documents deemed material or pertinent to the work of said Committee, and it is further

Resolved, that such Committee shall report to the Legislature with all convenient speed the result of its investigations with any legislation which it recommends, and shall make its final report on or before March 15, nineteen hundred forty-two. (*Report of the Subcommittee of the Joint Legislative Committee to Investigate Procedures and Methods of Allocating State Moneys for Public School Purposes and Subversive Activities,* Legislative Document [1942], No. 49.)

Appendix VII

The Feinberg Law

SEC. 3023. Elimination of subversive persons from the public school system.

1. The board of regents shall adopt, promulgate, and enforce rules and regulations for the disqualification or removal of superintendents of schools, teachers, or employees in the public schools in any city or school district of the state who violate the provisions of sec. 3021 of this article or who are ineligible for appointment to or retention in any office or position in such public schools on any of the grounds set forth in sec. twelve-a of the civil service law and shall provide therein appropriate methods and procedure for the enforcement of such sections of this article and the civil service law.

2. The board of regents shall, after inquiry, and after such notice and hearing as may be appropriate, make a listing of organizations which it finds to be subversive in that they advocate, advise, teach or embrace the doctrine that the government of the United States or of any state or of any political subdivision thereof shall be overthrown or overturned by force, violence or any unlawful means, or that they advocate, advise, teach or embrace the duty, necessity or propriety of adopting any such doctrine as set forth in section twelve-a of the civil service law. Such listings may be amended and revised from time to time. The board, in making

such inquiry, may utilize any similar listings or designations promulgated by any federal agency or authority authorized by federal law, regulation or executive order, and for the purposes of such inquiry, the board may request and receive from federal agencies or authorities any supporting material or evidence that may be made available to it. The board of regents shall provide in the rules and regulations required by subdivision one hereof that membership in any such organization included in such listing made by it shall constitute prima facie evidence of disqualification for appointment to or retention in any office or position in the public schools of the state.

3. The board of regents shall annually, on or before the fifteenth day of February, by separate report, render to the legislature, a full statement of measures taken by it for the enforcement of such provisions of law and to require compliance therewith. Such reports shall contain a description of surveys made by the board of regents, from time to time, as may be appropriate, to ascertain the extent to which such provisions of law have been enforced in the city and school districts of the state. (*McKinney's Consolidated Laws of New York Annotated,* Book 16, Part 1, Education Law.)

Index